OWL'S JOURNEY

OWL'S JOURNEY

Four Centuries of an American County

Maura D. Shaw

Illustrated by Joe Tantillo

S H A W A N G U N K

The Shawangunk Press
Wappingers Falls, New York

OWL'S JOURNEY: *Four Centuries of an American County.*
Copyright © 1994 by Maura D. Shaw. All rights reserved.
Printed in the United States of America. No part of this book
may be used or reproduced in any manner whatsoever without
written permission from the publisher except in the case of brief
quotations for purposes of review. For information write to The
Shawangunk Press, 8 Laurel Park, Wappingers Falls, NY 12590.

Except for identifiable historical figures, all the characters in this
book are creations of the author's imagination.

Text and cover design by Joe Tantillo.
Illustrations copyright © 1994 by Joe Tantillo.

Library of Congress Catalog Card Number 94-68193

ISBN 1-885482-01-9

First printing, September 1994.

10 9 8 7 6 5 4 3 2 1

♻ Printed on acid-free recycled paper.

Dedicated to Eileen Mylod Hayden, Director of the Dutchess County Historical Society, who formed my ideal of wit and kind intelligence when she taught my ninth-grade English class.

Contents

The Stone Owl

September 1609

Staring intently at the flat round stone cupped in his hand, the boy called Dark Moon barely heard the shouts of his brother and younger sister as they splashed in the shallows of the river around the bend.

The Lenape children had spent a long morning helping their mother with the corn harvest and were glad to be released to play. Dark Moon had walked by himself to the edge of the great blue river, where he intended to streak down the bank into the cool water like Brother Otter. But he was distracted by the glint of something pale in the muddy bank.

Picking it up, he saw it was a piece of weathered limestone about the size of his palm. He turned the stone over, feeling the smoothness of its surface and tracing with his fingertip the indentations worn into the limestone by wind and water and sand. The stone looked almost like an owl, if he squinted his eyes and used his imagination.

Dark Moon felt a kinship with owls. They were

such wise creatures and, like him, they could see through the darkness of the night. Dark Moon was not afraid of the deepest forest, where light could not penetrate even at the height of day, and he was not afraid of the darkest nights, when the moon was new and not even a silver crescent was visible in the sky.

To move through the night without hesitation was his special skill. His bare feet knew the shape of Mother Earth, and the roots of the trees seemed to move out of his path so he never tripped. He was not afraid of the birds and bats who hunted at night. He loved the long whooo of the owl and the sudden rush of its wings as it sailed to earth.

Dark Moon was twelve, nearly old enough to go on his sacred vision quest, when he would live all alone in the forest for three or four days. He hoped that he would meet his Guardian Spirits and learn from them how his gift of night vision was meant to be used. Dark Moon wondered if this stone owl had a message for him. At least, the stone looked like an owl—with his father's awl he could make the curves around the owl's eyes deeper, and maybe scratch some lines to suggest its feathery wings.

Hearing the calls of the other children, he slipped the stone owl into the deerskin medicine pouch that he wore on a thong around his neck. It was heavy against his bare brown chest, but it made him feel somehow special. He was eager to use the carving tools to bring the owl out of the stone.

He might have time tonight, when the family was

sitting around the fire in the longhouse made of oak bark, enjoying the smoky warmth and the satisfaction of full bellies. His father had been blessed by Mesingw, the Hunter Spirit, and had brought home two buck deer from his last hunting trip. His mother had been busy all week, cutting the meat into long strips to dry, rubbing the strips with berries and herbs, so that they would have food during the long hungry winter when game was scarce. But she had also kept some of the best pieces for venison stew, and a large pot of vegetables and meat was simmering over the cooking fire even now. Dark Moon's mouth began to water in anticipation.

It was only in the harvest time that food was so plentiful. Many nights in the chill winter he would lie on his sleeping furs feeling pangs of hunger, praying to Mesingw to send a plump rabbit or squirrel through the snow near their village—one who was willing to become a stew. He would dream of early spring, when the first green shoots brightened the wetland, and his mother would ladle generous scoops of boiled greens with wild onions and dried corn into their gourd bowls.

The memory of how good the dried corn tasted after a hard winter—and how their work in the harvest time kept the People alive to rejoice in another spring—helped Dark Moon to forget how sore his fingers became when he had spent all day shucking the dried kernels from the ears of corn. Corn, beans, and squash were the most important foods for the People; his

3

mother called them "the Three Sisters" and planted their seeds together in the same mound of soil.

Soon, though, he would be old enough to hunt game with the men and leave the garden work to the women and younger children. That would be a great day. To practice, Dark Moon swiftly and silently crept up behind his little brother on the riverbank and, quick as a hunting owl, scooped the child off his feet. Laughing, he ran with his brother into the rippling water and together they hunted for clamshells on the sandy bottom.

Dark Moon worked hard that evening, and a few more evenings as well, to carve the owl's likeness in the stone. At last it was done to his satisfaction. He showed it to his best friend, Blue Heron Boy, as they were watching the men of the village sharpen their spears and scrapers for the big hunt tomorrow.

"You made this yourself?" said Blue Heron Boy, as if he didn't believe it.

"I found the stone in the river and it looked like an owl," said Dark Moon. "So I tried to make it even more so."

"It feels like it's got good medicine—you know, sort of owl power," said Blue Heron Boy, swooping with imaginary wings. "Have you shown it to Turtle Woman?"

Dark Moon shook his head. He was more than a little in awe of Turtle Woman, an elder who healed the People with herbs and singing and dreamed about what was causing their sickness and how to cure it. She was a medicine woman and a storyteller. "Maybe sometime I'll show her," he said.

In truth, he wasn't sure that he wanted Turtle Woman to know about the owl. She often said that owls brought news of someone's death and she might not want an owl totem in the village. To change the subject, he sighed loudly. "Don't you wish we were going on the hunt? I'll bet I could get a black bear if they would only let us try."

Blue Heron Boy looked with longing at the sharp stone axes and quivers of arrows leaning against the longhouse where the men were working. Someday he would have his own deerskin quiver, decorated with dyed porcupine quills and beads made from mussel shells. He tried to wait patiently until it was his time to become a man, but it was awfully hard, especially on the eve of a big hunt. He practiced with his bow and arrows in every spare minute of the day.

"If you could get one black bear, I could get three! I would make a necklace of bear claws so heavy I couldn't stand up straight when I wore it!" replied Blue Heron Boy in a big voice. He loved to boast and never expected anyone to take it seriously.

One of the men heard him and laughed. "Are you sure you're strong enough, little brother, to shake even a deer claw rattle in the dance tonight?"

Blue Heron Boy ducked his head in embarrassment and the others chuckled.

The men of the Wolf Clan planned to travel into the far hills to hunt for several days, but before they left they held a sacred ceremonial dance to ask the Creator to send plentiful game to the hunters, so the People would be fed. Blue Heron Boy and Dark Moon were both looking forward to dressing in their best deerskins and leggings to be part of the ceremony. Dark Moon had a rattle made from the shell of a box turtle, which he had filled with dried cherry pits and mounted on a peeled stick. It was his favorite possession, until the day he found the stone owl.

Slapping his friend playfully on the shoulder, Dark Moon said, "Let's take our spears out for some practice throws in the cornfield." He knew it would cheer Blue Heron Boy to score a few direct hits on ferocious tree-stump targets.

It was the night of the new moon, when the sky was completely black except for a sprinkling of stars. The elders said that the trail of stars were the footprints of the People's ancestors on their way to heaven.

The hunters had been gone for five days, and in their absence Dark Moon and Blue Heron Boy were proudly playing their roles as the oldest males in the village—if you didn't count the grandfathers, whose time for hunting was past. The two boys circled around the longhouses after dusk, on the lookout for any hungry mountain lions who might be bold enough to snatch a puppy from the safety of the village. They didn't see any big cats, but the rustle of animals in the darkening woods gave them satisfying goosebumps as they shook their spears in the air.

From inside one of the longhouses they passed, the boys heard voices raised in alarm. A woman thrust open the door flap and rushed to the edge of the clearing, calling anxiously for her daughter. "Little Willow! Little Willow! Daughter, where are you?"

The three-year-old had been underfoot near the central cooking fire, so her mother had sent her to play outside until her supper of cornmeal mush was ready. Somehow the hours had gone by without anyone noticing that the little girl had never returned. She had wandered off alone into the forest.

The young mother and her sisters ran to Turtle Woman, who was sitting quietly near the fire in her own family's longhouse. Frantically they explained what had happened and asked for the medicine woman's help. Dark Moon and Blue Heron Boy listened from a respectful distance.

"Do not worry," said Turtle Woman, closing her eyes briefly and drawing a long breath. The shell necklace and copper bracelets that she wore gleamed dully in the firelight.

She tossed a small handful of dried leaves into the center of the fire and stared steadily at it, as if she could see pictures in the flickering orange and blue flames.

"A brave will go into the forest and bring back the child unharmed," she said. "The child is calling for her parents because she is caught between a slippery log and a great rocky wall. There is no light in the forest tonight."

The mother covered her face with her hands in anguish. "Our men are not coming back until tomorrow!" she cried. "My daughter is lost and she will not survive the night alone. She is only a baby!"

Turtle Woman looked at her with sympathy and understanding, but also with a little annoyance, because the young woman did not seem to believe the vision that Turtle Woman saw in the flames.

"A young man will find her and bring her back through the night," repeated Turtle Woman. "It is true. He is waiting here, behind us."

The old medicine woman rose from her blanket and slowly turned around until she was standing face-to-face with Dark Moon. Suddenly he realized that he had grown taller this summer, taller than Turtle

Woman, who used to tower above him when she shook her prayer rattles and sang her songs in ceremonies. He swallowed hard and tried to stand straight without looking nervous.

"You are the one we call Dark Moon," said Turtle Woman in a deep strong voice. "The Creator has blessed you with the ability to see through the night, and now you are being given a chance to use that gift to help this woman and her daughter, Little Willow. Are you brave enough to go into the deep forest, to the edge of the rock where the water falls, and carry back your little sister?"

Dark Moon had a flash of memory—the happy giggling of the child Little Willow as she played in the river shallows with his own small brother, splashing and pretending to be giant fish. Of course he was brave enough to rescue her!

"I will go immediately, asking the Creator to light my way there and back," said Dark Moon aloud, in as grown-up a voice as he could muster. Silently he prayed that he really would be able to find Little Willow and find his way home again in the dark night.

He looked over at Blue Heron Boy, whose eyes were open wide with surprise, and gently touched the deerskin medicine bag hanging on a thong around his neck. In the bag was the stone owl. The owl would help him.

Without delay Dark Moon prepared to leave. His own mother gave him a small bag of berries and bean cakes to share with Little Willow as soon as he found her, and a soft handful of spider web wrapped in a leaf, in case the little girl had been scratched or cut by the rocks. His mother ruffled the hair on top of his head as he said goodbye.

Blue Heron Boy accompanied him to the first turn into the dark forest. "You really know where you're going?" he asked, a little anxiously.

"If Turtle Woman's vision is true, then it's about two hours' walk to the waterfall. In the daytime, that is," he added. "It might take longer tonight."

"Travel safely," called Blue Heron Boy as Dark Moon's bare feet sped along through the brush.

He stopped before he had gone much farther and pulled the stone owl out of its hiding place. He clasped it tightly in his hand, feeling the warmth of the stone. Having the owl with him, hunting through the night for the little lost girl, was comforting.

Several hours passed in silent running, sometimes slowly through dense woods and sometimes faster, particularly when he heard noises in the undergrowth that were not made by the People. There was no sign of the child, and Dark Moon desperately hoped that she was still waiting by the waterfall. He didn't want to think of what would happen if she had freed herself and wandered forward to the edge of the cliff.

At last he saw her. Just as Turtle Woman had envisioned, Little Willow was lying with her leg caught in a hollow under a heavy tree. She was whimpering unhappily and her face was smudged with dirt. Dark Moon called softly to her, and she raised her head and smiled. After a few minutes he was able to free her by rolling the log away. It thundered over the cliff with a loud crash when it hit bottom far below. Dark Moon shuddered when he heard the sound.

The tired, thirsty child ate only a few of the berries from Dark Moon's pouch and then put her arms around the boy's neck. Dark Moon realized that she wanted to be carried home. Her leg was bruised and swollen from being trapped under the log for so many hours. Although it didn't look broken, he doubted whether Little Willow could walk all the way back to the village. Well, he would just have to carry her. She couldn't weigh more than a basket of dried corn.

The forest seemed even darker and the trail even longer on the way home, but Dark Moon felt the ground with his feet and peered through the night with his owl-like eyes. Once they heard a low deep growl behind them and Little Willow began to cry in fear. "Probably Brother Mountain Lion," said Dark Moon to himself and picked up his pace even more. He pressed the stone owl into the little girl's hand and told her to hold onto it because it brought good luck. The owl would guide them through the darkness safely home.

By the time Dark Moon reached the edge of the village, the dawn was breaking and Little Willow weighed at least as much as twenty bags of beans. The muscles in his arms and legs were aching and weary.

But when the little girl was reunited with her mother and Turtle Woman nodded to Dark Moon with approval, the smile on his face was hard to conceal.

Maybe he would show Turtle Woman the stone owl, after all, he thought sleepily. He might like to learn how to see the visions in the fire, if she would teach him the way.

He slept for a few hours, until the hunting party returned, laden with game bags and full of tales about the enormous bear that got away. When Dark Moon's father was told the news of his son's brave rescue, the hunter was clearly pleased. "Perhaps you are grown enough now to join us on the next hunting trip," he said, resting his hand on his son's shoulder.

"Blue Heron Boy too?" asked Dark Moon quietly, glancing at his friend standing near the circle of men.

"We'll see," said his father with a promising smile.

Later that afternoon, Dark Moon and Blue Heron Boy were lying on their stomachs on the high bank that overlooked the great river, chewing grass stems and telling stories about the great hunting expeditions that they would lead in a year or two.

Dark Moon was the first to spot the strange canoe rounding the curve of the river. It was larger than any dugout canoe he had ever seen and rode high above the blue water. What looked like great white clouds billowed above it and seemed to propel it forward in the stiff autumn breeze.

The craft was too far away for him to see what tribe of people were aboard, but he was sure it wasn't any of the Lenape clans.

"I wonder what it brings?" he murmured to himself

as he and Blue Heron Boy tore down the bank to tell the village about the huge canoe coming up the river.

The stone owl, tucked in his medicine bag, couldn't tell him.

In 1609, an Englishman named Henry Hudson sailed a Dutch ship called the Half Moon *all the way from Amsterdam across the Atlantic Ocean to the New World. He was searching for a northwest trading passage to the East, which was rich in treasures of spices, silk, and gold. Instead he found a great river, which now bears his name, and a population of gentle natives who welcomed him with food and gifts. He sailed as far north as Albany and returned to tell his employers of the treasure of furs, timber, and fertile soil that awaited the traders and settlers who came to America.*

Treasure in the Wilderness

June 1723

Anneke wiped her hot face with the back of her woolen sleeve and once again wished she were a boy.

Her brother Pieter was down at the gristmill, supposedly helping their father load the sacks of newly ground cornmeal into the canoe for the trip back home across the river. But Anneke just *knew* that he and the youngest Brett boy instead were off playing bows and arrows with their Indian friends.

The stone step where she crouched, shelling peas for dinner, was only partly in the shade of the tree near Mistress Brett's kitchen door. The heap of empty, bright green peapods seemed to be growing bigger, but when Anneke peered into the earthenware bowl that held the shelled peas, it didn't seem as if there would ever be enough to feed all the men and boys who were at the mill today.

"Too bad they can't eat the peapods, too," said Anneke with a sigh.

Mistress Brett, who owned the gristmill at the

mouth of Fishkill Creek, had invited Anneke and her brother and father to stay for dinner. Anneke was pleased. Just as she had promised her mother, she offered to help with the preparations. Secretly Anneke hoped that Mistress Brett instead might ask her to come along when she galloped out on her big horse to oversee her tenant farmers or visited with the native Wappingers tribe in their village. Anneke's mother had told her that Mistress Brett was a good friend to the Indian people and that the women even showed her how they wove colorful mats from plant fibers and sewed with needles made from deer bone. It seemed very exotic to Anneke.

Apparently Mistress Brett's reputation as a hard-working businesswoman was well-deserved. Almost before she knew it, Anneke was handed the basket of fresh-picked peapods—and no doubt the mistress would find plenty of other work for a ten-year-old girl to do. Anneke's cherished hope of a holiday from everyday chores quickly disappeared. But at least she was shelling peas somewhere other than her own doorstep.

A black servant wearing a turban poked her head out of the kitchen door. "Mistress says it's time to find Robert and Rivery and bring back the fish they caught for dinner."

Anneke jumped at the chance to escape from the endless peapods. She wiped her hands on her apron and trotted down the path toward the river some distance away.

As she got closer, she could hear the great grinding

sound from the mill as the huge round stones turned one upon the other, crushing the corn kernels into grist, and the whooshing and squeaking of the wooden waterwheel that powered the crankshaft to turn the millstones. Gristmills and sawmills were almost always built near swift running water, which provided both power and transportation. The spot where the Fishkill Creek emptied into the broad Hudson was perfect.

Anneke saw a few men and older boys in front of the mill, but she didn't see her brother or Robert or Rivery Brett among them. Several Indian men stood patiently with leather sacks of dried corn and tied bundles of furs. Anneke knew that sometimes they traded furs for having their grinding done. She was sure that the Indian girls—who used to grind all the meal with a stone in a hollowed-out tree stump—were pleased.

She walked upriver from the mill a little way until she spotted the three boys she knew and two Indian boys on the bank. All five boys were laughing as they skimmed flat stones across the surface of the water, each trying to outdistance the others.

"Looks like fun," said Anneke, feeling more than a little left out.

Pieter motioned her to come closer. A heavy woven basket of shining bass waited in the cool shade under a willow tree.

"Look, Anneke!" said Pieter in an excited voice. "These boys taught me how to catch fish with a spear! Just like they do!" His woolen breeches were rolled up above his plump knees and his feet were bare. He grasped a long flexible spear in his fist.

Spearing fish was not an activity that appealed much to Anneke, but she could see that her brother was enjoying it. And she knew how important it was to be able to catch fish to eat, summer and winter—not only for the natives but for the settlers as well.

"What a great number you've caught, Pieter!" said Anneke, to be nice.

She hoped she wasn't expected to lug that heavy basket all the way up to the house by herself. "Mistress Brett wants the fish now," she began.

"Then let's quit fishing and get the bows and arrows!" said Pieter. He turned to the two darker-skinned boys and pretended to draw an arrow back on a bow. They both nodded and smiled.

"I've got to get back to bagging the cornmeal," said Robert, the bigger of the two Brett boys. Their eldest brother, Francis, was sixteen years old and did the work of a fullgrown man at the mill—he wasn't able to leave even to go fishing.

"I'll help you carry the basket up to the house, Anneke," said Rivery, who was eleven. "I'll catch up with Pieter later."

Anneke was pleased. She liked Rivery, especially his unusual name. He had actually been born on the Hudson River, aboard the Brett family's sloop as they sailed home to Fishkill Landing from the city of New York, sixty miles south.

Anneke was curious about what a city looked like. She could ask Rivery if he had ever gone to visit his mother's family in New York—or New Amsterdam, as it used to be called by the Dutch. Rivery's father, Captain Roger Brett, had moved north with his wife to develop the property that she had inherited from her father, Francis Rombout. But Captain Brett had been drowned in a thunderstorm—struck by the boom of his sloop and knocked overboard—when Rivery was only six years old. Mistress Brett had been left to manage the huge estate on her own after that. She had never married again, unlike most other widows.

Pieter and the other boys left to find their bows. Rivery lifted one handle of the basket and Anneke the other.

"Heave ho!" he sang out in a deep voice like a seaman's. He grinned at her, his brown straight hair falling into his eyes, and suddenly the basket didn't seem quite so heavy.

After they delivered the fish, Anneke was resigned to going back to shelling peas or hulling strawberries or whatever other task she was assigned. At least she could occasionally pop a sweet strawberry into her mouth, she thought.

But Rivery hung around outside the open half-door, as if he wanted to say something without the servants overhearing.

"I have a secret fort in the woods," he whispered in a low voice. "It's cool and quiet and nobody knows where you are. I go there once in a while, when there's too much work to do." He jerked a thumb back toward the gristmill.

Anneke giggled. She imagined it might be difficult sometimes to be the son of a widowed mother as energetic as Mistress Brett.

"Want to come along?" Rivery asked.

Anneke looked at the dark kitchen door and thought about her brother playing with his Indian friends. "I probably shouldn't—" she said. "But I will!"

They headed down the slope away from the river and past a green cornfield, keeping to the edge near the forest where no one could see them from the house. After a few minutes they crossed a clear brook, by stepping on large stones protruding from the water, and came to a circle of tall hemlock trees, where the ground was softly covered in dry brown needles.

Rivery had constructed a lean-to out of long straight poles secured to the trunk of a large tree with vines. He had woven leafy branches and straw between the poles to make a thatched roof.

He gestured to Anneke to make herself comfortable and settled himself at full length on the ground. "There's no one to boss you around here," he said. "My brothers haven't found me yet."

He pulled a wad of cloth out of his pocket and unfolded it. "Cruller?" he offered. The fried cake was a heap of crumbled pieces.

"Thanks!" Treats were rare in Anneke's frontier farm life on the west bank of the Hudson, especially cakes with sugar. She licked the sweetness from her fingers.

"We almost never have sugar," she said. "Honey

19

when we can find a bee tree, though."

The sweet cake made Anneke thirsty. Leaving Rivery to enjoy his fort, she walked back to the brook. She knelt down to drink from her cupped hands and when she looked up, she was face to face with a black bear.

The bear was a youngster, weighing only about two hundred pounds, but he was three times the size of Anneke. He looked at her with puzzled curiosity from the opposite side of the narrow brook, where he had come to get a drink, too.

For a split second Anneke thought she might fall into the water in a dead faint. Then she tried to remember what her father had told her about bears. Was she supposed to make noise and frighten it off? Or was she supposed to walk quietly backward, away from the bear, without alarming it? Or was she supposed to climb the nearest tree? Or was that the absolute *worst* thing to do? The bear could climb trees too.

The bear didn't move and neither did Anneke. She was so close that she could smell its pungent animal scent.

She had to do something. "Go home," she said firmly, in the tone of voice she used with her small brothers. "Go on, go home."

The bear shook the water drops from his muzzle.

Anneke knew that he could tear her in two with those powerful white teeth she saw, but she swallowed hard and repeated, "Go home."

The bear looked at her peaceably, almost as if he

understood what she was saying. He turned away and lumbered heavily off in the opposite direction.

As soon as the bear was out of sight, Anneke's feet found a speed she never knew she had. In a flash she was back at the lean-to, shaking Rivery by the shoulder. "It's a bear! A black bear!" she told him urgently.

Rivery didn't seem the least disturbed. "He always comes around this time of day," he said calmly. "Sometimes I toss him a cruller or two."

Anneke couldn't believe her ears. "You have a pet bear?"

"He never bothers me," said Rivery. "I think he likes me."

Anneke looked at him as if he were crazy. "What if his *mother* comes too?" she demanded.

21

"Well, she hasn't yet. I don't think there's much danger."

"I think I'd rather go back to shelling peas, Rivery," said Anneke in a shakier voice than she wished. Maybe Rivery could talk to the animals but she wasn't sure she could pull it off more than once in a lifetime.

"Fine," he said. "On the way back I'll show you an old cave I found."

"Are there bears in it?" asked Anneke, only half-teasing.

Rivery shook his head.

The mouth of the shallow cave past the cornfield was almost hidden by brush. Unless you were looking for it, the opening appeared to be just a pile of boulders. Anneke looked carefully around for animal visitors before she got down on her hands and knees and crawled into the cave.

The floor was dirt but surprisingly dry. As her eyes adjusted to the dim light, Anneke began to see that the roof of the cave was a large flat stone. She leaned closer.

"Those are pictures carved in the roof!" she said.

Rivery had wriggled into the cave after her, a cramped fit.

"Aren't they great?" he replied, as proudly as if he had made them himself. "There's a wolf, and a turtle, and some kind of bird, I think. Indians must have made them."

Anneke edged a bit farther back to see the carvings,

almost touching the rear wall of the cave. She put her hand down to steady herself and felt something soft, like skin, at the base of the wall.

"Ahhh!" she cried, pulling her hand away and hoping it hadn't been a snake.

Gingerly she peered down. Wedged into a crevice in the rock was what looked like a piece of leather. "What's this?" she murmured to Rivery, prying it out with her fingers.

She had to tug hard on the object to release it from its hiding place. It was a small bundle of deerskin leather, creased and stiff with age. Anneke gently unwrapped it, holding her breath, while Rivery watched.

Inside the deerskin were five small beads of white wampum, a dried twig that crumbled as she touched it, and a round piece of stone.

"I wonder who hid this here?" said Anneke. "Maybe it's been in the cave for a hundred years."

"Someone's treasure," observed Rivery. "Let's look at it in the light."

Backing out of the cave, Anneke carefully placed the bundle on the ground in front of her and picked up the stone. Laying it flat on her palm, she laughed with surprise.

It was a stone owl! The round eyes and feathery wings were clearly visible in the limestone. She examined it carefully. Judging by the leather in which it was wrapped, the stone owl must have been very old.

"An owl! Incredible!" said Rivery. "I've never seen anything like it before."

"Then it definitely must not belong to one of Rivery's Indian friends," thought Anneke with relief. She was beginning to feel that she had found a real treasure.

"Do you think I can keep it?" she asked, hesitantly. After all, Rivery was the son of the property owner, and perhaps whatever was found on their land was owned by them.

"I don't see why not. Finders, keepers, you know." He handed the owl back to her. "I wouldn't mind having the wampum, though."

"Of course!" said Anneke. "And the deerskin, too." She tucked the owl safely into the pocket of her apron as they started back to the Brett manor house.

Anneke was surprised when Mistress Brett called to her from the front porch and asked if she would like to come into the house to visit for a little while. Anneke had never been invited inside before. Hastily she smoothed out her apron and shook the grass from the back of her skirt. Mistress Brett looked so attractive in her yellow-striped taffeta day-dress and soft white lace cap.

The foundation of the house was gray fieldstone and the outside was covered with cedar shingles, which had been split by hand. Inside, the four large rooms were framed with great dark beams hewn of timber. The walls were whitewashed and nearly smooth. It seemed very grand to Anneke, who lived in a one-room cabin made of logs.

Rivery led Anneke down the central hall into the

north room, used for receiving guests. It was cool and spacious, furnished with a desk, a table, and several chairs, much more elegant than the ones in Anneke's own house. An open cupboard in one corner held an assortment of pottery and pewter and a row of leather-bound books.

"This is where my mother writes letters and conducts business," offered Rivery. "I hardly ever get to come in here either. I wonder why she let us in today?"

"I thought that Anneke might like to see a treasure of mine," said a pleasant voice from the doorway. Mistress Brett was smiling.

"You know, we still live in such wilderness here," she said, reaching for a small carved box, "that sometimes I miss the fine things I had when I was your age and living down in the city. I only brought a few treasures here when I married, and once in a while I like to take them out and look at them. Especially when young girls come to visit." She and Anneke sat down at the polished wood table.

"It's wilderness, all right," thought Anneke to herself, recalling the bear she had met just an hour ago. She felt for the stone owl in her pocket.

As Mistress Brett opened the box, Anneke breathed a heartfelt sigh. Inside the box was a tiny pewter tea set, buffed to a lustrous sheen. The cups were only the size of acorns. There were round dinner plates, pitchers, jugs, and even little soup bowls with decorative handles.

"Go ahead, set them out on the table," urged

Mistress Brett. "Aren't they exquisite? I've had them since I was a little girl."

It was the first time in her life that Anneke had actually seen anything that could be called "exquisite." What a treasure! She touched the miniature teapot with deep admiration. Someday she would like to have a splendid home and a desk and a lovely tea set, a grown-up one, to entertain visitors. They would talk about important matters over tea. She couldn't imagine that the wilderness where she lived could ever become so refined, but, as her mother always said, you never can tell what the future will bring.

She reached into the pocket of her apron. "I have a treasure, too," Anneke said as she delicately placed the carved stone owl on the polished tabletop.

"Oh, it's beautiful. Simply beautiful," said Mistress Brett, picking it up in her slender fingers. "A real New World treasure. Wherever did you find it?"

Anneke looked at Rivery in alarm. She didn't dare give away his secret hiding places.

His mother laughed knowingly. "Rivery's always disappearing somewhere or other," she said. "He's as slippery as a river eel. And by some coincidence the sugar crullers always disappear at the same time."

She handed the stone owl back to Anneke. "You must come to see me more often," Mistress Brett said. "Ask your mother if you may. Do you suppose you might like to meet the daughters of my Indian friends?"

Anneke nodded happily, her hand closed around the stone owl.

Mistress Catharyna Rombout Brett brought many new settlers to Dutchess County, selling them acres of her rich farmland, and she remained a loyal protector of the native people who lived there. Her miniature pewter tea set is still on display in the house where she lived until 1764, which is now known as Madame Brett's Homestead. It is the oldest standing house in Dutchess County.

3.

A Pirate's Gold

December 1752

Hans was listening for the rumble of the heavy wagon rolling over the rough track to the barn as he expertly squirted milk in a steady stream into the bucket. Gerta was a good milker and rarely kicked over the bucket with her hind hoof, as the younger cows did. He was eager to finish the barn chores before his brother Jacob returned from the dock at Rhinecliff with the load of supplies. It was two days before Christmas and there was much to be done.

He heard the two horses neigh loudly as they reached their own turnoff to the barn track—they knew that fresh water and hay awaited them. Hans dashed out to be the first to greet the wagon.

"There won't be another boat docking here this winter!" called Jacob as he tossed the horses' reins to Hans and jumped down. "The river's already beginning to freeze. And so is my nose," he said, rubbing it with his mittened hand.

Hans began to unhitch the animals from the wagon. Their breath was white in the chilly air.

"Did you get the iron hoops we wanted? And the new spoke-shave from the blacksmith? Did you get a good price for the oak casks?" Jacob had apprenticed to a cooper in the village and was now beginning to sell the water-tight barrels and smaller casks that he had made in his own woodshop. He was teaching Hans to make sturdy buckets. "Did you get the sugar cone, too?"

"Hold on!" said Jacob, putting up his hands. "Patience!"

Hans led the horses into their stalls and returned to the wagon, trying not to look too eager.

"Yes, I got everything," said Jacob, "even the sugar and spices for Mama's baking." Christmas wouldn't be Christmas without her stollen, a sweet spicy fruit-filled bread. Mama's own mother had brought the recipe with her from Germany in the family Bible, although many years passed before she could obtain the sugar and other special ingredients to bake it.

"And I picked up something for you, too." Jacob pulled an object from his jacket pocket and flipped it through the air to Hans. He caught it easily.

"It's a stone." Hans looked in puzzlement at his brother.

"Look again, little brother," said Jacob.

Hans turned the stone over in his hand. "It's an owl! Who carved it? It's wonderful."

Jacob shrugged. "One of the sloops that came up from Fishkill Landing had our iron hoops as cargo. When I helped to unload them, I saw this little piece of stone wedged under a box in the hold. Nobody else seemed to want it, so I brought it home for you. Merry Christmas." He grinned. "Now put that bird away and help me unload this wagon."

Hans lay awake in his quilts that night, unable to sleep even though he was tired. The loft above the main room, where the older children slept, was unheated, and Hans knew that the water in the stoneware washbasin would be frozen solid by morning. His two younger brothers huddled close together for warmth, like sleeping puppies.

But it wasn't the cold that kept Hans awake. He had a big decision ahead. He held the small stone owl in his hand as he went over the possibilities.

Hans was turning thirteen next month, and his father had told him that it was time to choose his way in life. Jacob had begged to be apprenticed to the cooper when he was thirteen, but as the years went on he discovered that he missed the farm more than he would have imagined. "I can't bear being stuck in a dusty wood room all day long, when I'd rather be out with my scythe in the hayfield," he had told their father. And Papa had missed Jacob's strong arms and cheery humor, as well. So he let Jacob came back to the farm, where he could use his barrel-making skills to earn extra money for the family.

But that left Hans without a solid future. The farm was only twenty-five acres, too small to support more than one family. When Jacob married in a few years, he would bring a wife and then children to the farm,

30

and coming along behind Hans were his two younger brothers. They might want to stay on the farm, too. In Rhinebeck, the farms were leased from the Beekman family, who had first settled the area, and it was next to impossible to buy a small farm outright. The Beekmans liked to collect rents from their tenants and hold on to the land.

Quite a few younger sons of the families around Rhinebeck left to carve new settlements out of the wilderness to the west. If that were Hans's plan, then he would probably stay at home until he was twenty or so, learning how to run a farm. But Hans couldn't imagine himself alone in the forest, struggling to clear enough land to plant a crop and build a log cabin. Hans liked to be with people.

That's what he had decided. He wanted to own an inn on the Post Road.

He wanted the excitement of new travelers stopping by every day for cider or a meal and bed for the night. He wanted to hear the gossip and the news. He wanted to know what was going on in New York and Albany and maybe other places that he hadn't even heard of yet. And he wanted to serve his customers delicious food like Mama's venison stew and apple strudels.

The problem would be in convincing Papa that he could do it.

Hans had already taken the first step. He had offered to work at the tavern several miles south on the Post Road, sweeping floors and washing dishes and watering horses—whatever the innkeeper needed. He

didn't ask for any wage but only a chance to learn the business, with a place to sleep and meals in the kitchen. The innkeeper had agreed right away. Now if Papa would agree, Hans would start to work a week after Christmas.

"Well, boy," said Papa after Hans explained his plans at breakfast the next morning. "It sounds like you've made your decision without consulting with me first."

"I—I—I'm sorry, sir, I didn't mean to," stammered Hans. "I just thought it was a good idea. And I hoped you would approve—" His voice trailed off. He couldn't tell whether his father was angry or amused.

"You did, did you?" His father speared another

piece of bacon with his knife. "You're in luck. I do. Besides," he added with a twinkle in his eye, "when I stopped at the tavern on my way back from the mill last week, the innkeeper and I agreed on it."

Hans was flooded with relief. Although he would miss Mama and Jacob and the younger children, he was beginning an exciting new adventure. He would take the stone owl with him to remind him of home.

Two weeks later, Hans was almost asleep in the stable behind the inn, wrapped in two blankets and buried under a heap of fresh hay for extra warmth. The horses quietly whickered in their stalls.

Hans didn't mind the company of the animals. Every night there were different horses belonging to the travelers, and Hans imagined that they were sharing bits of news from the horses' point of view, just as their masters shared their own over tankards of cider in the tavern.

One of the horses, a big chestnut stallion, was a real beauty. He stood so high that Hans had a hard time lifting the handsome saddle from his back, but the horse waited patiently. In the kitchen, while Hans was eating his supper, the new cook had told him that the horse alone was worth more than a farmer earned in a year and that its owner was in fact a famous pirate traveling in disguise.

"How do you know that?" asked Hans, his eyes wide.

"I have my ways," replied the cook, rubbing his thumb and forefinger together as if holding a coin.

Hans sensed an unpleasantness behind the man's smile.

"Now don't you be telling what ain't your business," the man said gruffly. He ladled another spoonful of greasy stew into Hans's bowl. It certainly wasn't as good as Mama's, but Hans was awfully hungry.

Thinking about the pirate kept Hans from drifting off to sleep. He patted his woolen jacket to make sure that the little stone owl was still safely in his pocket. It kept him company when he felt lonely.

Then he heard muffled sounds from outside the stable door.

Two men entered the stable, their boots scuffing on the dirt floor. One held a lantern covered with a dark cloth to dim its glow.

"First the horse, then quick up the back way to his room. I'll wager all his gold won't save his life!" said a rough voice.

"I won't mind being the man that cuts the pigtail off Bold Ned!" boasted the other.

Hans realized three things at the same instant. The pirate guest was none other than Bold Ned, known as one of the fiercest pirates on the Caribbean! And the two men were going to rob and kill him and steal his horse! And one of those men was the greasy new cook!

Barely daring to breathe, Hans tried to think of what he could do to stop them. Because he was covered by hay in the corner of the stable, he hadn't been seen—which meant that he had the element of surprise on his side. He swallowed hard and tried to think fast.

What strength would a thirteen-year-old boy have against two cutthroats?

He heard the men saddling the big chestnut stallion and another strong black horse. They led them toward the stable door, talking in hushed voices.

How could he stop them? Pirate or not, an innkeeper couldn't let a guest be murdered in his bed. But if the robbers discovered him in the stable, they would finish him off first.

"I have to chance it," whispered Hans to himself. He thought he could get a clear view of the men as they neared the open door.

Stealthily he withdrew the stone owl from his pocket. Jumping from the hay, he hurled the stone with all his might at the cook's head. It struck him smack on the forehead and sent him reeling against his partner in surprise.

The other man recovered first and turned toward Hans. He was pointing the largest pistol that Hans had ever seen. The pistol roared, a smoky red explosion. The man shot again, a little wildly. The horses screamed in fear.

"Idiot!" shouted the cook. "You'll wake them all!" He lurched toward Hans with a shiny long knife in his hand.

"Stay where you are," commanded a tall figure in the doorway. It was the pirate Bold Ned, fully dressed, with a pistol in each hand.

Behind him stood the innkeeper, awakened by the gunshots.

"Are you all right, lad?" called the pirate.

"I'm fine, sir," replied Hans, his voice cracking.

The two thieves were speedily tied up and held for the sheriff. The horses were quieted and the household began to settle down.

"Just how did you stop them, Hans?" asked Bold Ned, leaning against the inn's railing, as cool as could be. His dark suit and white ruffled shirt weren't the least rumpled after the tussle with the robbers. His leather boots were polished to a shine.

"I threw my stone owl at the cook," said Hans. "My charm against feeling homesick, sir," he explained.

The pirate looked puzzled until Hans showed him the owl. He had crawled around in the dirt near the stable door until he had found it again, none the worse for wear.

"Why would you be homesick, lad?" asked Bold Ned. "Don't you live here at the inn with your family?"

"No, sir." So Hans told him all about his plans to learn innkeeping and buy a place of his own someday. The pirate listened thoughtfully.

When Hans fell silent, suddenly afraid that he had blabbered on too long, the man reached into his waistcoat and pulled out a small drawstring purse.

"You saved my life, Hans," he said, "and I am in your debt. To show my gratitude, here's a bit of change to put toward buying that inn when you're older." He handed the purse to Hans with a wink.

"Oh, thank you, sir!" said Hans, unable to believe his good fortune.

"I had best be on my way now, before daylight," said the traveler, picking up his heavy saddlebags.

"Tell me, sir," said Hans, unable to resist the temptation. "Are you truly the pirate they call Bold Ned?"

"What's your guess?" The man laughed as he swung up into the saddle of the beautiful chestnut stallion. He trotted past the gate and headed north on the road to Albany.

Hans watched him go, almost too excited to peek into the drawstring purse. Was it really stuffed with Spanish gold doubloons?

Wait until he showed them to Jacob, stuck at home on the farm.

Many travelers made the long journey by horse or carriage on the Post Road between New York City and Albany, stopping at inns and taverns along the way. Some may indeed have been pirates, as well as governors, politicians, merchants, and presidents. The Beekman Arms, an inn built in 1766 on the site of the Traphagen Tavern, has been serving guests in Rhinebeck for over two hundred years, and other taverns were open for business north and south of the village as early as 1706.

4.

The Owl Rides for Liberty

April 1777

Rebecca Ludington's father had a price on his head. Not because he was wanted for highway robbery or murder, but because he commanded the regiment of colonial troops in southern Dutchess County who were rebelling against King George of England. A British general had offered to pay 300 English guineas to any man who could capture Henry Ludington, "dead or alive."

Since the war for American independence had started two years ago, the militia had been practicing their drills in the Ludington's pasture. Most of the men were farmers who had never wanted to become soldiers. They didn't have uniforms and some didn't even have guns, but to defend their land and families and their right to choose their own government they were willing to fight and even die. Rebecca hoped that none of them would die. And she promised herself that even though she was barely fourteen, she would do the best she could to help.

Her sister Sybil was sixteen and even braver,

Rebecca thought. Hardly anything made Sybil lose her nerve. One night last year, their house had been surrounded by a party of men who planned to rush out of the woods and seize Papa, to hand him over to the British. Luckily she and Sybil had been standing sentinel at the windows, watching for any strangers who might approach the house. When Sybil saw the men lurking in the woods she realized that an ambush was planned.

As Sybil ran out to the woods to identify the Tories, Rebecca stood guard and helped her father make a quick escape. No one had tried to attack the house since, but one of the older children always stood sentinel at night.

Just last week, she and Sybil had been working out in the kitchen garden behind the house, loosening and turning the wet soil with their hoes to prepare it for the spring planting. Their younger sister Mary was clearing the dead leaves from the roots of the sage and rosemary bushes, which protected them from freezing during the winter. The fragrance of the herbs drifted in the sweet spring air.

Mr. Prentice, one of the local Tories who sympathized with the British, had just ridden by on his great black horse. Rebecca has seen him peering at the house from the road, hoping no doubt to catch Colonel Ludington with one of the rebel spies who kept him informed of the British troops' whereabouts. Papa was too smart to let that happen.

Suddenly Rebecca saw Sybil stiffen, her hand still

on the hoe. A barn owl had hooted in the woods beyond the garden.

They heard it again and looked at one another. It was Enoch Crosby's signal.

The spy must have very important news if he was daring to travel in broad daylight. Usually when they heard his signal it was after dusk.

"I wonder how far down the road Mr. Prentice has gotten," said Sybil in a very low voice.

Rebecca knew that Enoch would stay hidden until he heard the counter-signal. "I'll go see," said Rebecca. She ran to the front of the house and then forced herself to walk at a normal pace out to the road, so she wouldn't look suspicious. There was no sign of the Tory. Even the dust from his horse's hooves had settled down again.

She ran back to the garden to let Sybil know that she could give the "safe" signal. Sybil was very good at sounding like a barn owl too.

Like a shadow Enoch slipped from the forest, dressed in buckskins like those the Indian scouts wore. Sybil and Rebecca thought he was very handsome.

"I have information for the Colonel," Enoch said. "I've got to be quick, though—the redcoats are brewing more trouble up north and I need to keep my ear to the ground." Rebecca giggled. Enoch liked to pretend that his work was more fun than dangerous, although they all knew the truth.

The three conspirators went quietly into the dairy room at the back of the house. As Rebecca poured the spy a foaming mug of cold milk and cut him some bread and cheese, Enoch gave Sybil the coded message for their father. No British soldier would suspect that two young girls were the spy's main contact.

Within a few minutes, Enoch was ready to depart. Sybil went out to make sure the way was safe.

Enoch smiled at Rebecca and reached into the pouch slung over his shoulder. "I brought you girls a trinket," he said. "I was in a tavern up in Rhinebeck talking to some fellows when I found this lying under the table near my foot. Keep it for good luck!"

The spy pressed a flat stone into her hand and disappeared through the doorway.

Rebecca looked at the stone. "An owl," she marveled. "A stone owl." She could even see the feathers etched in the stone. It seemed very old.

Swiftly she cleared away the evidence of the spy's hasty meal and went out to the garden to join Mary and Sybil.

She couldn't mention the owl in front of Mary, so she had waited to show it to Sybil until later.

"I wonder where it came from," said Sybil. She ran her finger over its smooth surface.

"He said it was for both of us," began Rebecca. She didn't want to say the spy's real name aloud, even in the house. "We can share it."

"No, you keep it," said Sybil generously. "If I ever want to borrow it, I'll ask you." She laughed. "If I ever need especially good luck!"

Night had long since fallen on the Ludington farm.

The animals were bedded down in their stalls and the birds in the trees were silent. No owls hooted.

Rebecca and Sybil stood near the stairs with a rush lamp, its smoky flame wavering and flickering, on their way up to bed. Papa sat at the table working on army supply lists, occasionally shaking his head and holding the paper closer to the candle in order to see the figures more clearly. Mama was quietly knitting. The colonial soldiers always needed socks, and even young Mary at ten years old was expected to knit one pair a week in her spare time.

Suddenly the dog barked and a thunderous knocking sounded on the door.

"Henry!" cried Mama.

"Colonel!" shouted the voice through the door as Papa lifted the heavy wooden bar that secured it. "The British have burned Danbury and they're on their way here!"

The exhausted soldier nearly fell into the room as Papa opened the door in a hurry. Breathlessly, he blurted out the news. He had just ridden all the way from Connecticut, where two thousand British troops had come ashore and burned most of the town, destroying the American army's supplies of food, tents, and other necessities. Now they were marching west to Ridgefield. The messenger had been sent to rally Colonel Ludington and his regiment to help stop the approaching British and drive them back to their ships on the Long Island Sound.

Colonel Ludington slammed his fist into his other

palm in frustration. "I have no one to send to arouse the militia!" he said. "My son is away and I cannot go myself—I must be here when the men assemble!"

"I can go, Papa," said Sybil calmly.

Rebecca's mouth dropped open in surprise.

"Nonsense!" said the Colonel. "It's a job for a man! I wish your brother were here—"

"I can do it, Papa," Sybil insisted. "I'll take Star—she's such a strong mare and she knows the roads. I can leave right away and be back before morning." Sybil spoke bravely and stood as tall as she could, like a soldier. Still she didn't reach as high as her father's shoulders.

"You don't have anyone else," she pointed out, trying to sound respectful. "And I know where all your men live."

"There is great need for haste, sir," said the messenger urgently.

"All right, Sybil," said their father. "But mind you be careful and watch for British soldiers along the roads. I don't want you captured like that fellow Paul Revere up in Massachusetts."

Sybil ran for her heavy dark cloak while Rebecca went out to the barn to saddle the mare. She was pretty sure that Sybil felt more afraid of the night ahead than she was letting anyone know. Even so, Rebecca didn't think she could do what her sister had volunteered so easily.

Mounted on the horse, Sybil seemed even smaller. Her father gave her instructions in a soldierly tone.

Sybil felt proud. She kissed her mother goodbye and leaned down to hug Rebecca.

Impulsively, Rebecca pulled the carved stone owl out of her pocket and handed it to Sybil.

"Carry the owl with you," she said. "It will help keep you safe."

"Thanks," whispered Sybil, and with a flourish she galloped off through the darkness.

Everywhere a militia man lived, Sybil rode right up to the house and hammered loudly on the door with a stout stick. There wasn't enough time to dismount. She shouted her message and rode on. One after another, the men grabbed their weapons and headed for Colonel Ludington's.

It began to rain steadily but still Sybil kept riding.

Her voice was growing hoarse from shouting, but the thought of the British redcoats marching through the night kept her moving.

"Come on, Star," she urged the mare when the road was rough. "We can do it."

Once she thought she heard the sound of soldiers behind her. She guided the horse down into a gully and rode through the shallow stream for a while, so the troops couldn't follow.

After thirty miles, Sybil was so tired that she could hardly keep her seat. "Only ten more miles, Star," she said. She wished she could just close her eyes for a few minutes.

Nearby an owl screeched, successful on its hunt for small prey.

The sound brought Sybil awake with a start. "That's what will happen to me if I fall asleep," she thought. "The British could get me just like a baby rabbit."

She took the stone owl out of her cloak and clutched it firmly in her left hand. "Keep me awake, owl," she said aloud. And she continued to ride through the night.

The last few houses on the route had already been alerted, and the militia men were on their way to the Ludington farm. Sybil was on her way home, too.

When she rode Star wearily into the yard, it was near daybreak. The colonel and his regiment had just left for Connecticut, where they would join the other American forces.

Rebecca and Mama were waiting anxiously. It had been a long and frightening night for them, too.

"Precious girl," her mother whispered to Sybil as she helped her down from the tired horse. "You were so very brave."

Rebecca stood near the door with a mug of hot cider and a warm dry quilt to wrap around the shivering girl. "I'm proud of you, sister," she said. "And so is Papa."

Sybil smiled and opened her hand to drop the stone owl into Rebecca's palm.

"I needed especially good luck last night, Rebecca," she said. "I guess the owl must believe in liberty."

The Ludington sisters played a small but important part in the American colonies' struggle for independence. Sybil's courageous ride on the night of April 26, 1777, is commemorated on a stone road marker in Stormville. The British were chased back to the sea by an army of farmers, millers, blacksmiths, carpenters, and other citizens of New York and Connecticut, many of whom had never fought a battle before. Like Sybil and Rebecca, they believed in the cause of liberty and freedom.

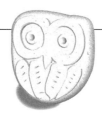

Circuses and Steamboats

October 1811

I t was just past the hour of noon. The autumn air was warm and a little sweet with the scent of apples. Eleven-year-old Will was so excited that he could hardly keep his feet still. He swaggered around in his new leather boots, kicking a green horse-chestnut clear across to the chicken coop and stirring up a considerable amount of dust. He even wore his Sunday shirt, although it was only Wednesday.

Isaac, the young hired man, had finished harnessing the big draft horses to the wagon, and Will's father waved to him to hop up into the straw-filled wagon bed. Will wasted no time. Today they were going to the circus!

The September harvest on the farm had been a good one. Will and Isaac had spent long hours in the fields, picking and hauling the bushels of corn and cutting the hay with sharp scythes. Every day they used pitchforks to toss the drying hay so it wouldn't get moldy from the rain, and every day they took their big cloth sacks to the orchard, filling them with apples and

47

peaches until the sacks were bulging and their backs were breaking.

The circus was their reward.

Will had seen the advertisements in the Poughkeepsie newspaper, full of exclamation marks and capital letters. They promised that CURIOUS townspeople and country folk alike would see WONDROUS CREATURES that few men ALIVE had ever BEHELD!!! The circus would be performing its show at Hendrickson's Inn on Market Street for two days.

The circus owner, a man from New York City, was going to exhibit an African Lion, the Mighty King of the Beasts. Will could only imagine what a lion's roar would sound like. But even more than the lion, he wanted to see the Indian Elephant from Bengal. And the Arabian Camels—two of them, the advertisement said.

There was a drawing of a tall animal with long skinny legs and a humped back, which Will guessed must be a camel.

The wagon trip into town took only an hour and a half. Will often went with his father to buy supplies or to sell their extra vegetables, fruit, and eggs. When they stopped at the dry goods store, he had his choice of a sweet or a biscuit from the tins on the counter. He almost always picked a hard sugar candy, because it lasted the longest.

Today, the market area was jammed with wagons, carriages, and horses hitched to the railing outside the inn. Will could hear the sound of a drum and a brass horn playing as he and Isaac and his father made their way toward the inn.

"Hurry, it's starting!" said Will, pushing forward through the crowd.

Will's father pressed a one-dollar gold piece into his hand. "Here, Will, pay your way in and find a place near the front where you can see. Isaac and I also have to see a man about selling our wheat crop, but we'll meet you at the wagon at suppertime. Be a good lad, now. And enjoy the show."

Will raced into the inn, dodging through the Poughkeepsie gentlemen and ladies dressed in their best clothes, following the sound of the circus music.

He edged as close to the circus ring as he could get, off to the side where the animal parade would begin. The air smelled heavy with damp straw, animal droppings, and cigar smoke—but there was a strange animal scent as well, which Will couldn't identify.

He leaned forward to peer around the corner into the tented area where the animals waited—and jumped in surprise. A boy about his own age grinned back at him. He was dressed in rough clothing and held a long thick rope in his hands.

The rope was attached to the most enormous gray-skinned beast that Will had ever seen.

The boy wrinkled his nose. "Elephants stink," he said. "But this here one's pretty gentle." He patted the huge creature's leg.

Will just nodded. The elephant had a long nose, which moved around as if it had a life of its own, and large floppy ears. Its feet were the size of tree stumps.

"C'mon back here," invited the boy. "You can watch the show from here."

Without hesitating a second, Will slipped into the tent. And then suddenly he wondered where the African lion was. Farther back under the canvas he saw a large cage on wheels, where a man stood with his back to the cage.

"That's my pa," said his new friend. "He takes care of the animals, and I help. My name's Sam."

The lion let out a powerful roar. Will heard the crowd outside shriek in anticipation. His heart beat fast, and the King of the Beasts roared again.

"Want to see him up close?" asked Sam. "He's pretty old, but he's still real strong. Could bite your head clean off," he said enthusiastically.

A man wearing a fancy suit of clothes came over and took the elephant's lead rope from Sam. "And the show begins," he said good-humoredly, with a flourishing bow to Will. To the sound of beating drums, he led the elephant out of the tent. Will followed Sam to the lion's cage.

The lion paced back and forth, swishing his tail. "Don't stick your fingers in," warned Sam. "That's one of the rules."

Will had not even been tempted to stick his fingers in. The lion's teeth were pointed and long. When he yawned, Will could see the reddish-purple inside of his mouth.

"We played a show last week in Connecticut," Sam said, although Will hadn't asked a question. He was completely fascinated by the lion.

"You know how we got from Connecticut to Poughkeepsie?"

Will didn't know, so he shook his head. He had thought the circus usually came up the river by boat from New York City.

"We walked. All the way. The elephants and the camels and all of us. Except the lion, of course, 'cause he could escape. That's why his cage has got wheels." Sam paused for dramatic effect.

"And you want to know the best part? We walk *at night.* You know, so the customers can't see the circus animals without paying their money for the show. We walk at night on the back roads, and we put big cloth sheets over the elephant and camels, with just their eyes showing, so nobody can peek!" Sam chuckled. "I'll bet there's some farm hands coming home late at night who think they've seen ghosts for sure!"

Will thought that was pretty clever of the circus. He wondered what kind of footprints the elephant left in the mud of the roads.

"Are the camels here today?" Will asked.

Sam nodded and motioned to the farthest corner of the tent. "You got to watch them 'cause they're mean," he said. "They'd nip you or spit as soon as look at you." He reached into his pocket. "We can go over there, but first I want to show you something I found."

Sam certainly talked a lot. Will thought maybe it was because he moved around with the circus all the time and had to make new friends in every town.

Sam opened his fist, palm up, and showed Will his treasure.

It was a flat round stone carved to look like an owl.

"We were coming over from Connecticut the other night, and I was leading the elephant. She doesn't like to go too fast, so to pass the time I was kind of scooting some stones around on the road with my foot as we walked," he explained.

"When I looked down, I saw this owl stone. Somebody must have lost it, I guess, on the Ludingtonville road. But I have it now. I'm going to bring it with me wherever I go," he said proudly.

"It's great," said Will, admiring the round eyes and beak. He had a feeling that the stone was very old. Sam put it back in his pocket for safekeeping.

Will could hear the oohs and aahs of the crowd outside as the elephant lumbered around the circus ring. Wouldn't any other boy give at least ten dollars to stand next to the lion's cage and be spit on by the camels, close up?

The camels looked so silly to Will, with their knobby knees, big lips, and furry brown humps, that it was hard to believe they were real animals.

Sam told him that the camels stored all the water they drank in their humps, so they could live in the desert, but Will didn't think that could be true. Sam also said that the Arabians put saddles on the camels and rode them as if they were horses, and Will thought maybe Sam was pulling his leg with that story, too.

But he was enjoying the chance to spend an afternoon with another boy, especially someone who led a life as interesting as Sam's.

Around four o'clock they heard a loud whistle from the river at the foot of Main Street. Will leaped up from the hay bale where he had been sitting, encouraging the elephant to pick up pieces of apple from his outstretched hand with her trunk.

"The steamboat!" he shouted.

Will was more interested in steamboats than in anything else in the world. He counted it a lucky day when a trip into Poughkeepsie coincided with a steamboat's scheduled run up the Hudson from New York City to

Albany, or back again. When he was only six years old, his father had taken him to see the first successful trip of Robert Fulton's *North River Steamboat of Clermont.* Will would never forget the sight of that mighty vessel steaming up the river, its belching smoke and noisy engine like a fiery monster among the sloops and sailboats.

He knew by name the six steamboats that operated on the river—the *North River*, the *Car of Neptune*, the *Trial*, the *Raritan*, the *Hope*, and his favorite, the *Perseverance.* Captain Elihu Bunker, who owned the *Hope* and the *Perseverance*, had set himself up to compete with Robert Fulton's steamboat company. They both incurred the wrath of the sailboatmen, who had monopolized the river trade for more than a century.

The new steamboats were noisy, dirty, and smelly. The pine knots they used for fuel in their boilers sent sparks and embers flying into the air, which burned holes in the sails of nearby sloops. But most of all, the sailboatmen hated the steamboats because they were faster. When the wind and tides were favorable, a sloop could sail its cargo from New York City to Albany in four days—but a steamboat could make the same trip in thirty hours or less. It made a big difference, especially for passengers traveling by boat.

The rivalry on the river was not friendly, and Robert Fulton had put oak guards around the big paddlewheels on the *North River* to protect them from being fouled by envious sloop crews who sailed too close to the steamboat. The sailboatmen rightly regarded the steamboats as a threat to the livelihood they earned by carrying passengers and freight up and down the river.

Graceful and sturdy as the sloops were, Will saw the promise of excitement and new opportunity in the brightly painted steamboats. He might want to be a boat pilot himself someday, he thought.

"Let's go down to the dock," suggested Will, lured by the piercing steam whistle. "Maybe they'll let us aboard for a minute."

"Or we could sneak ourselves on," said Sam, who was more daring.

The two boys ran down Main Street to the dock, where the *North River* was carefully chugging into its berth. As they watched, with a clang of bells the great steam engine sighed to a halt, and the crew tossed ropes to the men on the dock.

"She's quite a beauty, isn't she?" breathed Will. The boiler in the center of the boat was copper; the upper works of the engine were painted bright green and the paddlewheels brilliant red. The cabin and deck were ornamented with shiny gold and polished woodwork.

A dozen passengers disembarked with their baggage, and the steamboat hands began to load boxes and crates bound for destinations further north on the river. They were intent on their work. It was a matter of pride to keep to the thirty-hour schedule, or even to better it.

"Now's our chance," muttered Sam. Gesturing to Will to follow him, he silently maneuvered around the clutter of barrels and equipment on the dock and crouched behind a large crate.

"Are you crazy?" Will asked in a low whisper. "You're not really going to stow away on the *North River*, are you?"

"Watch me," replied Sam with a wink.

"The captain will have your hide when he finds you!"

"Naw, I'll just invite him to come to the circus tomorrow and bring the whole crew," Sam said with confidence. "You can bet he'll make some time in his schedule to see the Indian Elephant from Bengal!"

He took the stone owl from his pocket and closed his fist around it tightly. "Wish us luck on our adventure," he said happily, shaking his fist in the air. "And would you let my pa know that I'll be back tomorrow on the return trip, with company?"

Will nodded. What could he say? Don't go? Sam was a boy from the circus and pretty much did what he wanted, Will guessed.

"It was sure nice to meet you, Will," said Sam, and almost faster than Will could see, he slipped down the gangplank past the busy crewmen and onto the deck. He disappeared behind a stack of baggage.

The steamboat whistle blew and the bells clanged, signaling time for departure. Will stood there watching as the engine was fired up and a great plume of thick black smoke bellowed from the smokestack.

At any moment he expected to see the captain haul Sam by the ears from his hiding place and toss him down the gangplank. But there was no sign of anything unusual on board the steamboat.

The passengers waved to families and friends waiting on the dock as the great paddlewheels began to turn and the *North River of Clermont* resumed its speedy journey up the river.

Will waved, too—just in case the stowaway could see him.

As he trudged back up the hill, for a moment Will wished that he were the boy on the brightly lit vessel steaming steadily through the dusk toward Albany, instead of Sam. But his mood brightened as he recalled that he was on his way to Hendrickson's Inn, where his new friend the Indian Elephant from Bengal waited for apple pieces, and where his father would buy him a good supper before they headed home in the wagon.

Some other day he'd have a chance to board a steamboat, for sure.

When Robert Fulton and his partner Robert Livingston, of Clermont in northern Dutchess County, developed the first successful commercial steamboat in 1807, they opened a new chapter in the American transportation industry. By the 1850s the Hudson River and many other waterways were crowded with steamboats. Pilots challenged one another to steamboat races, and more than one vessel was blown to smithereens when its boiler exploded. Today steamboats are used for recreation and tourism instead of transportation—but people still thrill to the chug-chug of their engines and the unmistakable blast of the steamboat whistle.

6.

Friends on the Underground Railroad

July 1844

Phebe was proud to be an abolitionist. It was a big word for a ten-year-old girl to use to describe herself. What it stood for was even larger still—abolitionists were people who were trying to end the practice of slavery in America.

Although Phebe happily stood up in school and read the composition that she had written about why slavery was wrong, she kept quiet about what she really did as an abolitionist. That was because Phebe's house was a secret station on the Underground Railroad, which helped African slaves from the South escape to freedom.

Phebe lived with her parents on a small farm on the Oswego Road, near Moore's Mills. They were Quakers who lived a plain and simple life, centering around the Society of Friends' Oswego Meeting House at the top of the hill. Every Sunday the members of the Quaker community went to First Day services, dressed in their best clothes, and on Wednesdays they went to Fourth Day services, in their clean work clothes. In between, there were quilting bees and corn husking parties, and sledding down the hills in winter, and gatherings to welcome new babies. Phebe got to see her best friend Susan, who lived on the other end of the Oswego Road, pretty often.

But even Susan didn't know for sure that runaway slaves spent days and nights hiding in Phebe's barn. Phebe couldn't tell anybody—people's lives depended on her.

A peddler in Fishkill, Phebe knew, was an Underground stationmaster. Every day he walked through the village selling fish to his customers, letting them know of his arrival by blasts of the small horn he wore around his neck. But sometimes the peddler would blow a certain rhythm on his horn. To those who knew the code, it signaled how many runaway slaves were expected that night and the place of meeting. The abolitionists would meet the fugitives and guide them by moonlight along the back roads and fields to a safe house, often the Oswego station.

Phebe's father or one of the other Friends would hide the slaves during the day, give them food and drink and a safe place to rest, and then at nightfall lead them to the next station further north. Many of the runaways traveled as far as Canada before they felt safe from the slave-hunters. Even though slavery had been outlawed in New York State since 1827, an escaped slave could be captured and returned to his owner in the South. The slave-hunter would receive a reward and the slave would be whipped near to death.

Phebe shuddered just to think about it. She believed that all people were created equal and that it was immoral for one group of human beings to buy and sell another group whose skin color was different from their own.

Today was Wednesday, and Phebe was waiting for Susan and her family to arrive for the Fourth Day meeting. While the grownups discussed community business, the children gathered outside to talk and play quietly. Phebe and Susan, being older, sat under a shady maple tree to share news and keep an eye on the little ones.

"Wait 'til you see what I have," whispered Susan as her mother and father and her grown-up brother Stephen went into the long white meetinghouse. She patted the pocket of her gray skirt.

Phebe was curious. Susan was always finding oddities, unusual objects that seemed to attract themselves to her like a magnet. Once she had found an Indian arrowhead made from a glossy black stone unlike any that Phebe had ever seen before. Another time she had taken Phebe out into the orchard behind the gristmill and shown her a tree that had an iron shovel lodged right in the center of its trunk. The tree had grown around it, but Phebe couldn't think of any reason in the world why someone would leave a shovel in a tree for so long.

"I have a lucky stone," said Susan, settling down on the grass next to Phebe. "And you'll never ever guess how I found it."

Sometimes Susan's stories were as odd as her treasures.

"My brother went all the way to the river to fish for sturgeon this week," Susan began. "Honestly, I think he's sweet on a girl in Poughkeepsie and that's why he wanted to ride so far for some smelly old fish—"

Phebe grinned. Susan idolized her brother and didn't want him to get married and move away from home.

"Anyway, he brought back this *gigantic* sturgeon, which Ma cooked for dinner and there was so much that we ate it at every meal for three days. It must have been nine feet long. No wonder they call it Albany beef! If I never see another fish again it will be too soon."

"But what about the stone?"

"The stone?" repeated Susan, momentarily reliving the horrors of baked fish, fried fish, fish soup, and fish pudding. "Oh, the *stone*."

She reached into her pocket. "When Stephen cleaned and gutted the fish, he found this stone in its stomach. The sturgeon must have swallowed it."

Susan held it out to Phebe. "Look, it's carved like an owl."

Phebe touched it gingerly.

"Don't worry, he washed it," said Susan. "It must have been quite a mouthful, even for that huge fish."

The stone owl was smooth on the bottom, but on the top Phebe could easily see the owl's eyes and feathers etched into the stone.

"Stephen said it's a good luck piece. But not for the fish!" Susan laughed.

Phebe felt strangely drawn to the stone. It felt warm in her hand, and somehow familiar, as if she had been meant to have it.

"I like it a lot," said Phebe. "It's beautiful."

"You can borrow it 'til Sunday if you want," offered Susan generously.

When Phebe and her parents left the Fourth Day meeting, the stone owl rode comfortably along, wrapped in her handkerchief.

The moon was nearly full that night, which made it more dangerous for the family of runaway slaves on their way to Moore's Mills. Phebe helped her father fill the wagon high with fresh straw, which would conceal the runaways if they encountered any other travelers.

Many times her father went on foot to bring home people from the secret meeting place, but in this instance the fugitives were a mother, a father, and three young children. He knew that they would be exhausted, so he decided to risk taking the wagon.

It was hours after midnight when Phebe and her mother heard the creak of the wagon springs near the barn. They left their beds and, by the light of a candle, gathered together some biscuits and salt pork and pot cheese. Phebe hauled an oak bucket of fresh spring water from the well outside the kitchen door and carried it, with a tin dipper, to the barn.

Her father stood at the foot of the wooden ladder to the hayloft, holding it steady as a black woman carrying an infant wrapped in a shawl climbed wearily up the rungs. A young girl crouched in the straw nearby, her arms around a small boy. They both wore rough sleeveless shifts that looked to Phebe as if they were made from flour sacks. Their feet were bare and swollen from walking so many hundreds of miles.

"I'll carry Thomas," said the man, reaching out his arms for his sleeping son. "You go on up to your mama, Sally. We're safe for the night, thank God. And thank *you*, sir," he said, nodding his head to Phebe's father.

"It's the least I can do," he replied, with a sad smile. "Someday I hope this whole country will see slavery as the terrible evil it is and put a stop to it. In the meantime, we'll do the best we can to get you to freedom."

Sally looked at Phebe shyly as she stood up and shook the straw pieces from her shift. Phebe smiled and handed her the dipper filled with water. The girl drank thirstily and then lifted the bucket to carry it up to the loft.

"I'll get the food basket," said Phebe. At the top of the ladder she slid the basket onto the loft floor. "I'll bring more tomorrow."

The next day was very hot. Inside the barn, the family of fugitives rested from their long, difficult journey, building up strength for the last few hundred miles.

After Phebe's morning chores were done, she sat with Sally in the open doorway of the barn, ready to give a warning if any strangers approached the farm. Little Thomas chased the barnyard chickens, giggling when they squawked. He didn't seem any the worse for their ordeal.

Sally told her a few details about their desperate escape, but she seemed to prefer to look forward to her new life ahead.

"Yes, we walked all the way from South Carolina," she said in a voice too weary to belong to a ten-year-old. "The master, he was going to sell my daddy down the river to a fearsome place in Mississippi, where nobody lives more than a year, even a healthy 'un like my daddy. So we all struck out one night, with only the clothes on our backs, and figured we'd try to get free together or die trying.

"We walked over mountains and through forests—wherever we thought the slave-catchers wouldn't find us—and people were kind to us most all the way," she continued. "Sometimes we had to keep to the creeks, though, so the dogs couldn't track our scent through the water. I heard tell that some folks got to stay *under-*

water for days, 'til the dogs give up and leave."

She laughed, pointing to her threadbare shift. "I don't think this fancy dress could have stood up to the water that long," she joked. "I'd come out wearing my birthday suit."

Phebe looked at Sally, trying to judge her size. "I've got a summer dress that might fit you," she offered. "If you wanted to wear it, I wouldn't miss it, really."

The girl's face brightened. "I'm embarrassed to start my new life wearing a slave's flour sack," she admitted in a low voice.

"I'll go right now and get it," said Phebe. "And I've got a spare petticoat, too."

Phebe sighed aloud when she took the blue cotton dress off the clothes peg in her room. Telling Sally that she wouldn't miss the dress was a lie. It was her brand-new Sunday dress, which she had helped her mother sew together just last week.

She and Susan had bought lengths of the same fabric from the milliner's store, so they would have matching dresses this summer. She hadn't even worn it once. And Susan would probably be mad at her for giving it away.

But that couldn't be helped. Phebe would try hard to give the dress away with a happy heart.

When Sally emerged from the horse stall wearing the blue dress and petticoat, Phebe didn't have to pretend to be happy. She genuinely was.

"Daddy says that where we're going, I'll learn to read and cipher numbers," said Sally. "Maybe I can send you a letter sometime, when we're free."

Phebe suddenly had a lump in her throat. She swallowed. "I could show you how to write your name today, before you leave," she said. "Then you'll be a step ahead."

She fetched her clean writing slate and a piece of hard chalk.

"These letters spell Sally. S-A-L-L-Y." She drew them firmly on the slate and then guided the other girl's hand to make the shapes of the letters. Sally practiced the letters over and over, until she could reproduce them from memory. Phebe thought she learned it amazingly fast.

"You won't have any problem when you get to school," she said. "You'll be a teacher's pet."

Sally looked serious. "I don't want to be anybody's anything, ever again. I just want to belong to me." Then she smiled.

"I have another name, too," she confided. "My mama said the master called me Sally but she gave me a true African name. Yemaya." She said the name proudly.

"Can you spell out the letters for Yemaya? It means mermaid."

Phebe thought she could give it a try, and Sally/Yemaya spent the next hour practicing how to write her true name on the slate.

Word came in the evening that the family could move on to the next stop on the Underground Railroad, north toward Amenia, as soon as it was dark.

As they climbed into the wagon bed once again, Sally/Yemaya carefully tucked her blue skirt around her and covered herself with straw. Phebe knew that the danger was far from over for the runaways.

She watched as the wagon disappeared down the Oswego Road.

"Oh no," she said suddenly. And she reached into the pocket of her old skirt, hoping to find the small stone owl that Susan had lent her.

But she already knew it wouldn't be there.

Phebe had put the owl, still wrapped in a handkerchief, into the pocket of her new blue cotton dress so she wouldn't forget to return it to Susan on Sunday, when the girls were planning to wear their matching dresses to the First Day meeting.

Instead, the stone owl was taking a trip on the Underground Railroad.

Phebe hoped the owl would bring good luck to her new friend. And somehow she would explain to Susan what had happened to the stone and the dress. Maybe Susan's family also worked for the Underground Railroad—Phebe would ask her father when he came back tonight. It certainly would make the explanation easier.

The Underground Railroad helped many people to escape from slavery in the years before the Civil War. Perhaps its most successful conductor was Harriet Tubman, who led more than three hundred slaves to freedom. People of all faiths, all colors, and all walks of life worked tirelessly for abolition; in fact, the Oblong Friends Meeting on Quaker Hill in Pawling, Dutchess County, publicly advocated the abolition of slavery in 1767, nearly one hundred years before President Lincoln's Emancipation Proclamation declared that all slaves in the rebelling Confederate states were free.

Cave-in at the Iron Mine

August 1856

The mouth of the iron ore mine where Eddie stood was framed by heavy timbers, supporting the earth and rock above it. A tunnel led into the mine shaft below, where it was always dark. Eddie's father was a miner, and even though he was only twelve, Eddie worked at the mine too.

One of his jobs was to bring buckets of water into the tunnel for the men. The opening was wide enough to haul out big carts filled with red-streaked rock, which contained the iron ore. Eddie's father and the other miners used drills to bore holes into the rock walls of the tunnel, and then they hammered metal rods into the holes as wedges, until the iron ore split off in chunks. Sometimes they needed to chop at the rock with pick-axes. It was hard labor.

The temperature inside the mine mouth was cooler than outside. It had been a sweltering hot August, and Eddie's arms and face and the back of his neck were tanned a deep bronze color from working out in the sun. When he took off his straw hat at night, he could see a band of pale white skin at the top of his forehead, where the sun hadn't reached. His mother teased him, calling it his angel's halo.

"Where's that water, Eddie?" called Skunks, the mine foreman. He had earned his nickname years earlier, when he had met up with a couple of skunks in the woods on his way to see the charcoal maker. The collier had smelled him coming from fifty feet away, and, in the tunnel the next day, all the miners threatened to quit unless Skunks burned his clothes and took a bath in the creek. Skunks no longer smelled but he couldn't get rid of the nickname.

"Right here, sir," said Eddie. He set down the buckets he carried in each hand.

Sometimes Skunks let him take the buckets down into the tunnel shaft himself. He wouldn't have minded today, since it was so blasted hot outside.

"I need you to run over to the shed and bring back half a dozen drill bits," said Skunks. "They're snapping off today like they're made of peppermint stick."

"Yes, sir," replied Eddie, disappointed.

He liked the exciting feeling of going down into the shaft, each step taking him further from the surface and the everyday world above.

The miners brought thick candles to light the tunnels, sticking them to the rock with melted candlewax. At the end of the workday they left the candle stubs where they were, for the rats to eat.

For the most part the miners didn't mind the rats. The rodents seemed to know, by some sixth sense, when a cave-in was about to happen and streamed out of the mine shaft by the dozen. When the rats fled, the miners weren't far behind. Eddie's mother told him that the coal miners in Pennsylvania brought small canary birds into the mines with them for safety, because coal gas would kill the bird before enough gas built up to suffocate the men or cause a mine explosion. Eddie thought that coal mining was even more dangerous than iron ore mining.

Eddie walked in no real hurry across the work area in front of the mine mouth and headed over toward the foreman's storage shed. A few of the men who were hauling wagonloads of iron ore to the smelting furnace waved to him as he passed. Even the mules were moving at a faster pace than Eddie was today.

He looked down at the big blast furnace, built against the hillside. A bridge reached from the storage shed to the top of the wide chimney. The men were loading a charge into the furnace, dumping layers of limestone, iron ore, and charcoal into the chimney from their wheelbarrows on the bridge.

A roaring hot fire in the furnace would heat the iron ore charge to more than 2,000 degrees, until the pure iron melted and separated from the impurities such as sand and carbon. The molten iron would flow out a tap hole at the bottom of the furnace and into sand molds in a casting shed, where it cooled into bars of heavy metal called pig iron. The impurities combined with the limestone into a material called slag, which was drawn off through another opening in the furnace and discarded onto the slag heap.

The pig iron bars were carted off in heavy wagons to be shipped by boat down the river to New York City, although more often now they were loaded onto freight train cars. Skunks had told him that the pig iron from the mine was used to make cannons for General Washington's army in the Revolutionary War. Eddie was impressed.

He found the metal drill bits in the shed and started back toward the mine mouth. The August sky above him had darkened and ominous rumblings of thunder were getting louder. In late summer there seemed to be a thunderstorm nearly every afternoon.

Eddie flinched as a crack of white lightning sizzled in the sky. As it started to rain, he dashed toward the shelter of the mine.

He was almost there when he heard a rumble and crash that was louder than thunder.

Out of the mine ran a river of rats.

"Cave-in!" yelled Eddie. He was screaming at the top of his lungs and didn't even know it. "Cave-in!"

A cloud of dust billowed from the mine mouth, and Eddie could see a dozen men stumbling blindly out of the mine. They tumbled over one another in their haste to get out of the deadly tunnel.

Men dropped their tools and wheelbarrows and came running from all over the mine site.

Eddie reached the mine mouth just as the roof collapsed.

The timbers split into a jumbled heap of rocks and dirt, sealing off the exit. The skies opened and drenching rain fell.

Eddie saw his father helping another miner to his feet. Pa was all right, and Eddie sighed with relief.

A miner named Charlie was the last man to leap to safety through the crumbling tunnel.

"Skunks!" Charlie cried. "He was right behind me! Skunks!"

The foreman hadn't made it out of the tunnel in time.

"God help him," said one of the other miners in a hushed voice.

"We'll help him too," shouted Eddie's father. He started digging at the pile of rubble with his bare hands.

"Skunks! We'll get you out! Hold on, man, we're digging!"

Frantically the men pulled the timbers free and tore at the rocks, trying to open an air passage into the mine. They called his name again and again, hoping that he was alive to hear them.

Eddie worked along with the rest, soaked with rain and sweat. The water ran into his eyes and hid the tears that were falling as he dug. He had known Skunks since he was born. Skunks couldn't be lying in the mine, crushed under a ton of rock. Not Skunks. Eddie knew it couldn't be true.

His fingers bled from scraping at the rocks, trying to lift them from where the door had been.

It seemed like hours before one of the men shouted, "Hurrah! We're through!"

"Skunks! Call out, man! Are you hurt?" another shouted through the opening in the rubble.

Eddie's father kept on prying the huge boulders away from the mine mouth with a crowbar.

Eddie held his breath. Was Skunks all right?

They heard a faint voice coming through the rock.

"My shoulder's caught under a beam, that's all. I can't dig out to meet you fellas." The foreman's voice had never seemed so welcome to Eddie.

"Just sit tight, Skunks, we're almost there," called Charlie.

When they carried Skunks out of the mine, under the layer of rock dust his face was white with pain. But he smiled at the cheers and whistles of the men.

"It's not the first cave-in I've been in, and it's probably not the last," he said in a joking tone as he held his injured shoulder. "But you're a good lot, all of you, to get me out so quick."

Skunks turned to Eddie. "It's a good job that I didn't send *you* down into the shaft with the water buckets, son. You had a near miss this time."

The foreman looked down at Eddie's raw and bleeding hands. "And it seems like you did a hero's job, too."

Eddie didn't know what to say.

"But where the devil are those drill bits I sent you for?" Skunks asked in a ferocious voice. He winked to let Eddie know that he was teasing.

"I must have dropped them when I heard the crash, I guess. I'll find them, Skunks," he said.

The men took Skunks off to his cabin to get some whiskey for the pain. Charlie said he would ride to Amenia to see if the doctor was on his rounds there today—otherwise he would have to travel all the way to the doctor's office in Poughkeepsie.

Tomorrow they would see how much damage had been done to the mine shaft and maybe start digging another tunnel into the iron ore deposit, from a different direction.

The rain had stopped, and Eddie walked back to look for the drill bits he had dropped.

A light-colored stone was lying in the mud near the rubble of the cave-in. It caught Eddie's eye and he bent down to pick it up, wincing as he moved his sore fingers.

"An owl!" he said aloud in astonishment. It was a small flat piece of limestone, carved in the shape of an owl. He could just make out the owl's round eyes and beak under the layers of gritty dirt. He wondered how he could have missed seeing the stone earlier.

He dunked the stone in a puddle to rinse off the mud. "It's even got feathers! I wonder where it came from?" He had heard rumors that runaway slaves escaping from the South sometimes hid from slave-catchers in caves or mine tunnels in the area. Maybe a runaway had dropped it.

Eddie thought he might adopt the stone owl as his good luck piece. He would show it to Skunks tomorrow. Certainly Skunks would agree that luck had been with them today.

During the 1800s there were nearly thirty iron smelting furnaces in the eastern part of Dutchess County and iron ore mines that dated back to the earliest colonial times. The ruins of a number of them can still be seen today. When the American colonies declared their independence from England in 1776, the furnaces and foundries quickly mobilized to produce the cannons and ammunition needed to win the war. In peacetime the iron was made into farm tools and machinery and household items such as cooking pots, skillets, and stoves.

8.

Abraham Lincoln's Ghost Train

April 1865

Bridget and Jimmy were frequent visitors to the railroad station in the city of Poughkeepsie. The engineers on the steam locomotives pulling the heavy freight trains saluted them with clanging bells and short bursts of the train whistle. Sometimes the people looking out the windows of the passenger trains waved to them. The two children always waved back.

Jimmy's father was a brakeman on the New York Central's Hudson River Railroad line. Six days a week he traveled by train back and forth from New York City to Albany. Bridget's father worked in the Railroad Restaurant, where passengers waiting to board trains could have a bite to eat. He was the assistant cook, and Bridget's mum helped out by baking pies for the restaurant.

Jimmy Ryan was Bridget's best friend. His parents had come over from Ireland during the Great Famine, fifteen years ago. Mrs. Ryan said that people in the old country were starving to death because the potato crop failed too many years in a row, and rather than eat grass and die of it like the family down the road, she

78

and Patrick Ryan had packed their bags and set out for America. Mrs. Ryan was only sixteen years old then, and now she had a great son almost twelve years old who was an American citizen, besides. Bridget liked Mrs. Ryan.

Bridget wasn't yet an American citizen, because she had been born in Ireland. She could barely remember the long sea voyage from County Clare in the West of Ireland, five years ago when she was only six. When they landed in New York City, people told them that up north, in Dutchess County, there was land for farming and jobs on the railroad, so here they came. Da's job at the restaurant was only temporary, until he got his feet on the ground and a good word at the railroad office.

The big excitement at the railroad station today was the arrival of the Ghost Train. That wasn't what the newspaper printed, of course, but that's what Jimmy and Bridget called it. President Abraham Lincoln—who Jimmy said was the greatest president of all time—had been shot dead in Washington, D.C., and his funeral train was passing through Poughkeepsie on its way to his final resting place in Springfield, Illinois. Mr. Lincoln became president the same year that Bridget had arrived in the United States.

The newspaper on April 15, ten days ago, had printed the horrifying news in big black letters: "Awful News! President Lincoln Assassinated. He is Shot through the Head. He was at Ford's Theatre. He is Dying."

Mum had started to cry when Da read the headlines aloud. "Oh, the poor man!" she wailed. "And the war just over! He didn't even live to see the good that he done."

The War between the States, which people called a Civil War, had ended only five days earlier, when General Robert E. Lee of the Confederacy surrendered to General Ulysses S. Grant of the Union forces. Jimmy Ryan's uncle had been killed in the war, at a battle called Gettysburg.

Bridget had seen the Union soldiers riding the trains, in their uniforms of dark blue and gold. Jimmy's uncle had been proud to serve his new country. But Bridget was sorry that he was never coming back—he had been full of jokes and was always mimicking Father Murphy, the parish priest, 'til you thought your sides would split from laughing.

Now, Bridget and Jimmy were helping to drape the Railroad Restaurant with black mourning for the slain president.

"Abraham Lincoln was a good man," said Bridget's father solemnly. He measured off a length of black crape fabric to hang in swooping folds over the doorway. Even though he was sad about President Lincoln, Bridget had the feeling that he truly enjoyed decorating the outside of the building with dramatic black festoons to mark the importance of the funeral train.

"He'll be sorely missed. And the fellow that shot him—an actor named John Wilkes Booth—hasn't yet been captured. There's a $100,000 reward posted. I don't think he can get far, though, seeing how he broke his leg escaping from the theatre after he shot Mr. Lincoln."

Whistling cheerfully, he stood on a ladder to adjust the folds to hang evenly.

Bridget's job was to tie big bows with black and white satin ribbon. Jimmy attached the bows to the porch railing with thin wire.

"What do you think—would a nice black drooper from the second-floor window set it off just right?" Bridget's father asked them. "Jimmy, I could hold onto your feet and you could hang out the window upside down to pin on the bows—"

At the alarmed look on Jimmy's face, he laughed. "Sure, I was only kidding, boyo," he said. Bridget wasn't so sure that he had been.

The three stood back to admire their work.

"Still seems a bit drab, hey?" said her father. He went into the storeroom at the back of the restaurant and brought back an American flag. They tacked it over one of the windows.

"If Mr. Lincoln hadn't kept the South from seceding from the Union, this flag would have been torn in half," he declared. Bridget's father read the newspaper every day and was studying books about the history of his new country. Bridget knew that he didn't mean the flag would actually tear. He was talking about the country being divided into North and South.

"Come back to the kitchen for some tea and buttered bread," said Da. "Your empty stomachs must be sticking to your backbones after all that work." Bridget giggled. He always said that.

Bridget and Jimmy hung around the freight yard for the rest of the afternoon, watching the huge locomotives bringing in cars loaded with brick, bars of pig iron, coal, and milk. Most of the freight was bound for New York City.

Sometimes interesting objects fell off the cars as they moved through the railroad yard. Bridget collected pieces of coal to burn in the stove at home, and once she found a chipped mug bearing the New York Central's name, which must have come from a dining car. Jimmy had found the best, though, last week. It was a small round stone that looked like an owl, with wings and eyes and a beak carved on its surface. Bridget wished that she had seen it first. Jimmy kept it in the pocket of his pants.

People from all over Poughkeepsie started gathering at the railroad station. The Ghost Train was due to arrive at seven-thirty, on its way north to Albany. Even the city merchants were closing their shops at six-thirty to demonstrate their respect for Mr. Lincoln.

By seven o'clock the crowd numbered in the thousands, a mixture of well-dressed citizens and rough-clad laborers. Bridget saw her mother with Mrs. Ryan on the bridge over the tracks, their black shawls matching the drapes on the building. All the rest of the children—Jimmy's younger brothers and sisters, as well as Bridget's—were gathered close around them, holding onto their skirts. Bridget waved, but Mum didn't see her.

A party of ladies waited by the platform, carrying beautiful wreaths of flowers.

"That one's the Mayor's wife," said Jimmy, pointing. "I'll bet she's going to go right into the private car where the coffin is."

Bridget felt a shiver run down her spine.

"Do you believe in ghosts, Jimmy?" she asked, making a hole in the gravel of the yardbed with the scuffed toe of her boot. She peered up at him.

Jimmy had climbed high on the rocks along the track and was perched on a ledge barely wide enough to hold his skinny frame.

"Nah," he replied. "Ghosts are a bunch of blarney."

"I heard a banshee once," said Bridget. "When my grandmother died, I heard it scream right outside my window. Do you think that haunts like banshees can cross the ocean?"

"No, but I think ghosts can ride on trains!" said Jimmy in a spooky voice. "And here it comes!"

The deep low tolling of the steam engine's bell could be heard around the curve in the railroad track, coming toward the station.

Bridget felt the hair on the back of her neck prickle. It sounded so sad, so mournful.

A split second later, she heard a crumbling, sliding sound as the ledge on which Jimmy sat suddenly gave way.

In a tumble of stones and dirt, Jimmy sprawled across the train track. The breath had been knocked out of him by the fall.

"Jimmy!" Bridget ran to where he lay.

"Are you killed?" she cried.

Jimmy shook his head and sat up. The mournful tolling of the huge bell continued as the locomotive drew closer. Bridget felt the bell was her heartbeat.

"I'm not dead yet but I will be if I don't get off these rails," said Jimmy in a scared voice.

"My foot's twisted. Here, pull on my leg."

Jimmy's foot was trapped between the iron track and the cinder bed, wedged against a railroad tie.

"I can't move it," said Bridget. "Your boot is stuck."

The engine was in full sight now, moving slowly toward them. It was the escort engine, ten minutes ahead of the engine pulling the nine-car funeral train.

"I don't want to be run over by a ghost train!" screamed Jimmy. The engine looked enormous, completely covered in heavy black cloth with an American flag on either side of the smokestack.

Bridget's fingers flew as she tugged at the knotted boot laces, trying to loosen them.

"Hurry! Pull your foot out of the boot—" Bridget commanded.

The engine shrieked a warning whistle.

With a jerk, Jimmy's foot came free from the boot. Bridget grabbed his hand and they jumped to safety, running back into the freight yard.

"Quick! Hide behind the water car!" said Jimmy. He was afraid of what his father would do if the engineer recognized and reported him.

Within seconds the massive engine rolled over

Jimmy's abandoned boot, crushing it completely.

"That could have been your head, you idiot," said Bridget.

"My ma's going to kill me for losing my boot anyway," said Jimmy dolefully. "I'll have to make up a story to tell her, or else my father will kill me double for acting so foolish in the freight yard."

Bridget looked up the track at the platform. All the men and boys had taken off their caps or tall hats as the first engine pulled ahead of the station. The crowd stood in complete silence. Only the tolling of the bell could be heard.

"Shhh. Here it comes," she whispered.

The second engine rolled toward them, its bell tolling in unison with the other. It too was hung with black cloth, even the brass railings, looped with silver eagles and silver tassels and satin ribbons.

On each side of the cab where the engineer sat was a portrait of President Lincoln, shrouded in black crape and satin. The cowcatcher in front carried a flag and even the headlights were draped in black crape.

"Jeez," said Jimmy.

The passenger car carrying President Lincoln's coffin was even more magnificent. It was the last car to pass Bridget and Jimmy on its muffled wheels. The outside was covered in black crape, with clusters of silver stars bordered in silver fringe. On the center panels were the words "United States" and a group of flags and shields, with an eagle above them.

"Your father would love to get his hands on a bit of

that silver tinsel for the restaurant," said Jimmy, making a feeble attempt at a joke. He couldn't bear the weight of grief and sadness surrounding the train and the people who came to honor the great man who had died.

Bridget didn't say a word. On the platform, a band played a slow funeral dirge. A few people emerged from the train and went into the Railroad Restaurant. "Da must be thrilled," Bridget thought.

Fifteen minutes later the big steam locomotives hissed and squealed and slowly the Ghost Train began to pull away from the station. It was growing dark.

"I want to find my Mum," Bridget said to Jimmy.

She felt an uncommon loneliness and thought she would like to have Mum's strong arms around her in a hug.

"I'll just get my boot, then," replied Jimmy. Peering carefully up and down the track, he scooted out to retrieve the shredded leather boot. Not much was left.

Jimmy looked at it, then at Bridget. "You're a grand girl, Bridie," he said. "Maybe I can return the favor sometime."

Bridget snorted. "I hope *not*! Only a blithering idiot would get his foot stuck in a railroad track."

Jimmy took her hand and pressed a small round object into it. Even before she saw it, Bridget knew it was the stone owl.

"I want you to have it," Jimmy said. "With my undying gratitude." He swept his cap off in a deep bow, like a stage actor.

Bridget laughed.

Jimmy tossed the ruined boot into the underbrush. Then he leaned over and took off the other boot. With a grin he hurled it into the scrub trees that lined the track.

"What's the use of a single boot? It will only make it harder to come up with a good story for my ma."

Together, the children walked toward the bright lights of the Railroad Restaurant.

During the second half of the nineteenth century, many families of immigrants came to Dutchess County from different parts of Europe. The Irish were among the first, and, because they already spoke the English language, they were able to find employment as railroad workers, police officers, firefighters, farm hands, and household help. They were quick to embrace the democratic spirit of America and participated enthusiastically in the political process, in local, state, and national government.

9.

A Snowy Owl in the Great Blizzard

March 1888

It had begun to snow, lightly at first, but within a very few minutes the wind had picked up and the flakes were coming down with fierce purpose. Matthew stood at the window of the farmhouse and watched the storm build. The snow was mounting faster than he had ever seen it before.

By the time he went out to the barn for the afternoon milking, the drifts of white powder were up to his knees. He and his father and the two dairymen, Frank and Lester, worked steadily to milk the rows of cows in their stalls. The dairy farm had close to a hundred cows, and the milk they produced was sent all the way to New York City from Pawling on the train.

"The girls are skittish tonight," muttered Frank as yet another cow shied away from the touch of his hands when he went to milk her. "Must be the storm coming in."

"There, there, Alice dear," he said gently to the cow. Sometimes Matthew wondered if Frank had been kicked too many times in the head.

"Certainly looks like a big one," agreed Matthew's father. "But you never know—it could fizzle out entirely by morning. It's a little late in the year to have a blizzard." In fact, by the calendar's date, spring would arrive in ten days, although the ground was still frozen hard as rock.

The snow continued all night, with raging wind and bitter gusts. Small drifts blew in through cracks in the window frame and piled snow on the floor near Matthew's bed. When he got up in the pitch-black dark to feed and water the cows, which was one of his daily chores, he heard unusual noises downstairs in the kitchen. He pulled on his clothes and raced down.

His parents were standing in front of the back door, which opened into the mudroom behind the kitchen. A wall of blank white filled the doorway, as tall as his father's chest. Matthew thought he must be seeing things, or else he was still asleep.

"Snow's almost as high as the doorframe," said his father. "We'll have to dig our way out to the barn."

His mother bit her lip anxiously as she looked from window to window. "All you can see is white, white, and more white," she said. "I've never seen a storm like this." The wind howled.

"Can't we just push our way through it, Pa?" asked Matthew.

His father shook his head. "You could get lost in a snowbank that deep, son, and we wouldn't find you for days. If you didn't smother, you'd freeze to death."

Matthew and his father took the coal shovels and

began at the top of the snow, as high as they could reach. The iron shovels were heavy and left black coal streaks in the clean white snow.

It took them hours to shovel a path wide enough for one person to get to the barn. As they got closer, they could hear the cows lowing unhappily in their stalls. Their breakfast was late and their udders were uncomfortably full. When Matthew looked behind him, he could see that the path near the house was already beginning to fill up with snow.

Matthew shoveled another path to the well and began to pump fresh water into buckets for the cows. "Hope they like ice water," he joked to his father as he carried the buckets into the barn.

Frank and Lester arrived a little while later, after digging themselves out of the tenant house they shared down the road. The two brothers were covered with snow and icicles hung from their mustaches.

"Nothing's moving out there," said Lester. "The snow's too deep for a sleigh."

"Maybe you fellows should bunk here in the barn tonight," suggested Matthew's father. "It doesn't look as if it's letting up any."

After the milking and feeding were done, Matthew went inside to eat his own breakfast, and the three men strung a rope from the barn to the back door. You couldn't see three feet ahead of you in the blizzard. Holding onto the guide rope was the only safe way to go between the two buildings.

Before long, it was time to clear the path again.

Matthew's shoulders and arms ached from shoveling, but he didn't dare complain. Keeping the herd of dairy cows alive was more important than a sore muscle or two. The cows were their livelihood.

Late in the afternoon, the heavy snow was still piling up. It was above the windows now, and Matthew began to be afraid that it would never stop.

"The milk trains can't get through, can they, Pa?" he asked.

"No, there's too much snow on the rails. When the blizzard stops, the railroad will have to send out crews to shovel the tracks." He shook his head. "We're going to have to put all this week's milk outside to freeze before it sours. I don't know if the dairy company will want it by the time we can get it to them, though. The poor young'uns in New York City are already crying

for their milk by now, I'm afraid."

The grown-ups' voices were serious as they talked at supper that second night. The storm showed no sign of letting up. At least they had plenty of food and fuel, but there was no chance of leaving the farm until the snow stopped, with milk cans or without.

Frank and Lester thought it best to sleep in the barn, so they could do the morning chores without having to shovel their way in again.

"Could I stay, too?" asked Matthew. He thought it might be fun to sleep on the hay bales. Maybe Frank would tell stories to pass the time. And besides, he was growing very tired of playing checkers with his eight-year-old sister and giving horsey rides to his three-year-old brother. Anything would be better than that.

"Would Matthew be a help to you, Frank?" asked his father.

Frank grinned. "The manure is sure mounting up in the stalls," he said. "Matthew could be in charge of mucking them out."

Matthew's face fell.

"He's only joshing, Matthew," said Lester. "We cleaned the stalls earlier this afternoon."

Bundled with blankets and well supplied with water and food and kerosene lanterns, the two dairymen and Matthew spent the night in the barn. As Matthew had suspected, Frank was a first-rate story-teller, but what he hadn't known was that quiet Lester could top any story that Frank could dream up. He was the King of Tall Tales.

"How did you learn all those stories?" asked Matthew, yawning sleepily.

"When I was young I worked on a riverboat down the Mississippi," replied Lester. "The crew used to tell each other the biggest whoppers I ever heard, and I can still recall most of them to this day." He smiled, remembering. "Did you know that there's a man by the name of Mark Twain who writes books about the riverboats? You might enjoy reading *Huckleberry Finn*, Matthew," he said. But Matthew was already asleep.

Matthew spent the next day as well with Frank and Lester in the barn. The snow was now over a dozen feet deep. The day was a long blur of pitching hay to the cows and lugging buckets of oats to the horses, milking, drawing water, and shoveling. Then it had to be repeated all over again.

While they warmed their frozen toes around the coal stove in the kitchen at midday, Lester taught Matthew to whistle the "Star-Spangled Banner."

Frank, not to be outdone, showed Matthew how to write messages in Morse code, which he had learned in the army.

"You know, Samuel F. B. Morse lived right here in Dutchess County," said Frank with pride. "I saw his original telegraph machine once."

Matthew looked impressed, and Lester loudly began to whistle "Oh! Susanna" with great gusto.

After supper the three trooped out to the barn again for the night.

"Maybe it's my imagination, but doesn't it seem to

be slowing down?" asked Matthew, looking up at the gray-black sky.

"I heard about a blizzard out in Kansas that lasted for two solid weeks—" began Frank.

Lester chuckled. "That's nothing. A really *good* blizzard will snow all the way 'til July," he said, and the storytellers were off and running again.

The most exciting event that happened in the barn on the third night of the Great Blizzard was the birth of a litter of kittens to the old black cat. Matthew decided to name the single all-white kitten Snowstorm.

When they awoke to the mooing of the cows at dawn, the snow had tapered off to flurries. Sixteen feet of snow covered the ground, twenty feet in some of the drifts. There was a powerful lot of digging-out to do, but life on the farm would soon return to normal.

As Matthew picked up his shovel to clear the path to the well pump again, Lester reached into his vest pocket with one hand and put his forefinger to his lip with the other, signaling conspiracy.

"There's something I want you to have," Lester said in a whisper, so Frank wouldn't hear. "I found it years ago near the railroad tracks in Poughkeepsie, and now I'm going to pass it on to you. To remind you of the good times we had, stranded here in the blizzard."

Lester handed Matthew a small round stone.

"Gosh!" exclaimed Matthew. "It's an owl! Look, it's got feathers and everything! Thanks, Lester!"

Lester smiled with pleasure. "Guess it's sort of a snowy owl now," he joked.

"I'll keep it forever," vowed Matthew.

"What's taking you so long, Lester?" called Frank from the barn door.

"Not a thing, Frank. Not a thing," replied Lester, with a wink.

The Great Blizzard of 1888 crippled the entire Northeast for the four days that it snowed and for some days thereafter, as city dwellers and farmers alike had to cope with the forces of Mother Nature. Shopkeepers dug tunnels from their doors out to the street to keep their businesses open, and practical jokers perched their hats atop twenty-foot snowbanks along the sidewalks, as if they were completely buried in snow. Modern snow-removal equipment did not exist—the roads and walkways had to be shoveled by hand. And without radio, television, or weather satellites, there was no way to know ahead of time that such a tremendous blizzard was on its way.

10

When the Whistle Blows

October 1906

Domenica squeezed her eyes tightly shut and pretended that she didn't hear her mother calling. She was so warm and comfortable that she wanted to snuggle under the bedcovers for at least another hour.

"Domenica! The coffee is ready and you must hurry if you want your breakfast this morning!"

Mama had that edge to her voice that she got when she was too rushed and too tired. She must have stayed up late nursing the sick baby down the hall. All the neighbors called on Mama when they were ill, and most times she knew just what kind of tea to brew or what ointment to rub on their chests to help them get better. But it didn't make it any easier for Mama to get up early in the morning to go to work at the factory.

None of the neighbors could afford to go to the doctor. They lived crowded into one or two rooms in the brick-and-frame houses off West Main Street in Wappingers Falls, even the families with nine or ten children.

Most of the families that Domenica knew had come over by boat from Italy, the same as she and her mother had. Domenica's father worked as a steward on one of the ships, traveling back and forth from the old country to the new. They only saw him once every few months. The money that he earned was being saved to buy a farm across the river, while Domenica and Mama worked in the Sweet-Orr overalls factory to earn their living. Her older brothers and sisters were still in Italy, living with Nonna, their grandmother, until Papa could afford to quit the shipboard job and settle in America for good.

With a loud sigh, Domenica threw back the covers and reached for her clothes, which she had piled on the chair last night. She washed her face in the basin and sat down at the table to drink her coffee. She liked it with lots of sugar and milk. Sometimes she dunked her bread in the coffee, too.

Mama hurried around the room, straightening the beds and picking up Domenica's nightdress from the floor.

"Get your shoes on," said Mama. "The whistle's going to blow any minute."

So many people in the village worked for the factory that a loud steam whistle was blown to signal the start of the day's first shift, the noontime break, and the evening dismissal. Domenica didn't want to be late—if she was, she would lose money from her pay envelope at the end of the week.

She and Mama separated at the factory gate. Mama went to the big room where her sewing machine would soon be humming steadily, stitching the heavy blue denim into pairs of overalls. The factory produced a thousand pairs of "never-rip" overalls each week. Farmers and laborers all over America wore them every day.

Domenica went to the cutting floor. She worked as a runner, carrying stacks of fabric pieces from the pattern cutters to the seamstresses all day long. A few other children worked there too, delivering finished overalls to the pressers and keeping the supplies of buttons well-filled. At the noontime dinner break, the children gobbled their bread and cheese and fruit quickly so they would have a few minutes to play outside.

Domenica looked forward to the games. They played hopscotch and marbles and kick-the-can, happy to be free from the adult world for a little while. Domenica had a secret wish that she prayed for every night, before she went to sleep. She wished that she could stop working at the factory and go to school instead, like most of the other girls whose fathers already lived in America.

The hopscotch court in the factory yard had been washed away in last night's rain. Serena, Domenica's friend, drew another long rectangle on the pavement with tailor's chalk. Domenica looked around on the ground for a stone to use for a marker.

Over in the corner of the yard, against the iron fence, was a small flat object, light-colored and easy to see. It would be perfect. Domenica reached down and picked it up.

The stone was carved in the shape of a small owl, with wide round eyes and a beak. There were deep-scored lines that made the owl's feathers. Domenica thought it was almost magical.

"Serena, look what I found!" she called. Quickly she picked up another stone to use for hopscotch. She wouldn't want to chip the owl by tossing it onto hard cement.

She turned to run back to Serena and all of a sudden she was lying on the pavement, looking up at the sky.

For a moment she was dazed. Her head must have banged when she fell.

"What happened?" cried Serena. "I just turned my back for one second—"

Domenica tried to smile. "I guess I tripped," she said. "Maybe on my shoelace. Or on the wet leaves. I'll be okay in a minute."

Her left ankle felt funny, almost numb. In her hand she still clutched the stone owl. "Some good luck," she muttered. But she tucked the owl into her skirt pocket anyway.

"Can you still play hopscotch?" asked Serena in a hopeful tone.

The other girl held out her hand and Domenica awkwardly scrambled to her feet.

"I don't think so," she said. "I don't know if I can even walk. My ankle is starting to hurt."

"How are you going to work the rest of the day? Maybe I should get your mother to come out."

Domenica shook her head no. "They'll dock her pay if she has to leave her machine," she said. "If you can help me walk to the door, I think I'll be all right."

The steam whistle blew shrilly. The noon break was over.

"I'll help you as much as I can this afternoon," whispered Serena, as Domenica hobbled with her into the brick factory building. "I'll carry some of your loads with mine, whenever I get a chance."

Domenica looked at her friend gratefully as Serena hurried up the iron staircase. She mounted the steps slowly, holding onto the railing and trying not to put any weight on her injured ankle.

The afternoon dragged on. Domenica's ankle swelled until she had to loosen the laces on her shoe completely. She tried hard not to limp as she passed her mother's sewing station. Only once did she hide in a corner and cry from the pain. Reaching for her handkerchief, she discovered the forgotten stone owl in her pocket. Holding it seemed to make the pain less severe.

Domenica had never been so glad to hear the shutdown whistle blow its sharp blast. She hobbled slowly out to meet her mother waiting on the sidewalk outside the factory.

Mama knew instantly that something was wrong. She insisted on looking at Domenica's ankle immediately. Domenica was embarrassed to roll her woolen stocking off, where anybody could see her bare foot, but Mama wouldn't budge until she did so.

Her gentle hands felt cool on Domenica's warm, throbbing ankle. "I don't think it's broken," Mama said. "Probably a sprain, which hurts even more sometimes. Why didn't you call me out when it happened?" Mama sounded more upset than angry.

"I knew you had to stay at your machine," Domenica said. "We need the money."

Mama spat out a stream of words in Italian that Domenica didn't quite understand—ending with something about how an eleven-year-old should be allowed to be a child in a free country like America, not work in a factory like a laborer. A child should be able to go to school.

Then she said, more calmly, "We'll get you home and put a compress on that ankle. It should be fine in a few days."

Domenica leaned on her mother for support as the two began their slow walk home. As they turned the corner onto Main Street, Mama straightened up and peered into the growing darkness. A familiar figure was striding toward them, whistling and waving his hat in greeting.

Papa had come home, after four months away! Domenica wished that she could run and throw herself into his arms, but she had to wait until he reached them for her hug.

"What's this? The little one is hurt?" Papa's face became like a thundercloud.

"Your daughter is too young to work in a factory all day," said Mama in a fierce voice. She hadn't even said hello. "She needs to go to school. I won't allow her to go back to that job." Mama stood with her hands on her hips and her mouth in a straight line.

Papa threw his hands up and laughed. "Of course, of course!" he said happily. "Neither of you has to go back to the factory, ever. I am here in America for good, now. The other children and Nonna will be arriving in New York at the end of next month, and we'll all be a family again."

"Oh, Antonio," sighed Mama. "It's about time!" And she burst into tears right there on the street.

Papa picked Domenica up in his strong arms and carried her the rest of the way home, telling her about the treats that he had brought from Italy—hard salami, and provolone cheese, and chocolate, and candied fruits—until her stomach rumbled aloud. Her ankle didn't hurt half as much as it had.

Perhaps the stone owl in her pocket *was* magical. Her secret wish had come true.

The hard-working immigrant families who came to Dutchess County in search of a better future kept alive the traditions of their native countries as they adapted to their new American homes. Many of them found jobs in factories like the Sweet-Orr overalls factory in Wappingers Falls. And as the twentieth century went on, laws were passed to protect children from working in hazardous conditions and for more than a certain number of hours per day. Eventually those protections were extended to adult workers as well.

11

High above the Hudson

May 1929

Angel loved airplanes. He loved the way they looked, with their sleek lines and shiny paint. He loved the way they sounded, as they taxied down the field and buzzed off into the sky. He loved the way they smelled, a heady mixture of engine grease and gasoline fuel.

More than anything, Angel wanted to fly.

His father teased him about it. "Angel, would you want to be a stonecutter if I had named you Pedro instead of Angel?" he asked. In Spanish, *piedra* was the word for stone.

"No, Papa, I just want to be high up in the air like you," Angel would reply. And his father would laugh and give him a nickel for ice cream. Angel saved the nickels until he had enough to buy the new issue of *Flying* magazine, which he would read from cover to cover.

Angel's father worked on the construction crew that was building the new bridge over the Hudson River in Poughkeepsie. Because he had no fear of heights, he was able to climb easily along the catwalks suspended high above the river. Nothing was too high or too dangerous for Papa. He had been working on the bridge for four years now, ever since the family had come here from Puerto Rico in search of work.

Perhaps the bridge would be completed by next year, he said, and then he would find a job building something else. Poughkeepsie was growing by the minute.

The new bridge would carry automobiles and delivery trucks much more efficiently than the ferry boat that ran between Beacon and Newburgh. There was the railroad bridge, of course, but only trains could run on it. When Angel had climbed up to the top of the trestle on a dare, he could see between the wooden ties down to the river below. It would be more than a dare was worth to walk across the mile-wide river—and if a train rumbled onto the bridge, where would you jump off? Even Angel didn't want to fly without an airplane.

The closest Angel had gotten to a real plane had been last summer, when a pair of barnstorming pilots had put on a show outside Poughkeepsie, in a flat field off New Hackensack Road near the old Dutch church. He and his younger brother Miguel and Harold, who lived next door, had bicycled all the way from the north side of the city on the day Angel had seen the posters advertising the show in a store window.

"It will be fun," Angel promised them. "The barnstormers do aerobatics with their planes. Sometimes they have parachute jumpers."

The other two boys thought that Angel was a little too crazy about airplanes, but they agreed to go along.

There wasn't much else to do in the city on a Saturday—and if they loafed around, their mothers would put them to work beating the dust out of the carpets or weeding the gardens in their back yards.

By the time they got to the field, Harold and Miguel were more interested in flopping down on the grass with boxes of popcorn and paper cups of lemonade sold by the vendors than in watching the airshow. But Angel was in heaven. A silver Curtiss racing biplane was already in the air, looping high above them. He squirmed through the crowd of bystanders until he was so close he could almost touch the second airplane, preparing for its ascent.

The double-wing biplane still on the ground was a Stearman, Angel knew, gaily painted in red and black. Its engine hummed happily, and the pilot waved to Angel in a half-salute as he began to throttle forward. He wore goggles and a leather flying cap buckled under his chin. Angel thought he looked like one of the flying aces in *Wings*, a movie about the fighter pilots in the Great War that he had seen four times so far.

In the rear cockpit directly behind the pilot sat a woman passenger, wearing a bright blue flight suit. As Angel watched, the red airplane sped down the field and lifted into the air, gaining altitude every second.

The silver Curtiss buzzed over the field again. Angel felt his heart leap into his throat as he saw it suddenly plunge, nose down, toward the crowd. At the last possible instant, the plane pulled up out of the dive and headed straight up toward the sky again. Then the two airplanes circled around the field, in opposite directions, and it looked to Angel as if there would be a head-on air collision when they met. He almost couldn't bear to look.

Whoosh! Both planes tore upward through the air, belly to belly, then split and came swooping down again in matching arcs. They flew over the field toward one another at high speed, veering ever so slightly apart when they met that Angel could swear one airplane's wingtip passed under the other's. Angel thought he had never seen anything so exciting. They circled and then zoomed at full throttle over the field in the same direction, one plane positioned directly above the other, and then the silver plane rolled 180 degrees and flew back upside down about ten feet above Angel's head. It took his breath away.

"How could you fly completely upside-down?" he asked aloud.

The man smoking a cigar next to him replied, "Harnesses, kid. Strapped in."

Angel nodded. But it didn't really answer his question. How was the pilot able to have such control over the plane that he could fly it with the ground above his head instead of the sky?

The silver plane accelerated high into the air and did two loops before landing smoothly on the grassy field.

The red Stearman, still in the air, flew steadily over the crowd and Angel opened his eyes wide. The woman in the blue flight suit was standing outside on the lower wing of the plane, waving enthusiastically to the spectators below. She was a wingwalker!

Angel had read about wingwalkers who did all sorts of acrobatic tricks in the air, including standing on their heads. As Angel watched, the woman climbed up the struts onto the upper wing and sat down on top, dangling her feet over the edge as if she were sitting on a garden wall. She perched there through a series of barrel rolls, loops, and spins—Angel couldn't take his eyes off her, for fear she would tumble to the ground—and then she gracefully resumed her standing position on the lower wing for the landing. When the plane stopped, she hopped off and bowed to the applauding crowd. Then she strolled over to a large signboard, which read "Airplane Rides $1.50." A line of customers quickly formed, the wingwalker collected the money, and once again the two biplanes were in the air.

"I wish I had the money," said Angel to Harold. "I'd give anything for a ride."

"It was a pretty good show," agreed his friend. "But you couldn't earn that much money in a month. And back home in Alabama, we could eat for a week on it." Harold's family had come north only last year, looking for opportunities that would provide a better living than sharecropping cotton in the south, where they lived from hand to mouth no matter how hard they worked.

"Harold's right," piped up Miguel. "You shouldn't do such dangerous stuff without telling Mama."

"Go home, Miguel," said Angel. But of course Miguel didn't. Little brothers were such pains-in-the-neck.

The boys hung around the field for another hour, watching the two planes take passengers up for a ten-minute flight and land again to pick up the next passengers without a break. Miguel was complaining that he was too thirsty to ride his bicycle home, but the boys had no more money left to buy lemonade.

"Look around on the ground to see if somebody dropped a nickel," suggested Angel. "You might get lucky."

Miguel took his suggestion seriously and scoured the field where the crowd had been standing as they watched the aerobatics show.

"No nickels," he said with disgust after a few minutes. "But I found this stone. Want to see?"

He held out a flat piece of limestone in the palm of his brown hand.

"It looks just like an owl."

"Let me see," said Angel.

"You can keep it. You're the one who likes things that fly," said Miguel, dropping the owl into his hand. "I really wanted a nickel."

"I'll buy you an ice cream when we get home," promised Angel, happy to sacrifice part of his savings for such an interesting object. "You, too, Harold," he said, feeling generous. It wasn't every day you found a stone owl.

Angel had kept the owl in a cigar box under his bed since that day last summer, with his chewing gum and his collection of airplane pictures torn from magazines. He still hadn't managed to get his first flight, although he had saved $1.50 in coins from his job selling newspapers on the corner of Main and Market streets. But the barnstormers hadn't returned. Papa said it was because the government was cracking down on such dangerous flying, and now pilots had to have licenses and safety inspections of their planes.

Sometimes he still bicycled out to the field on Saturday. There was some talk about turning it into a real airstrip, and Angel didn't want to miss any of the action.

Today the weather was cool and clear—a perfect day for flying. Angel decided to try his luck at the field again. He tucked the stone owl into the pocket of his short pants, for good measure. Harold and Miguel were playing ball at the corner lot and weren't interested in biking out to an empty field, so Angel went alone.

No one was there when he arrived. But it was a beautiful day to do nothing—Angel walked to the middle of the field and stretched out on the grass, looking up at the blue sky. Only a few soft clouds floated high above the earth. He heard the whirring of the insects in the field and the chirping of the robins in search of worms.

And then he heard the engine. A purring, roaring sound that was unmistakable—a plane was circling the field to land, right where he was lying!

Angel jumped to his feet and shaded his eyes with his hand, straining to identify the plane.

"A racing plane!" he cried. "It's a Travel Air!" The graceful lines of the airplane became clearer as it descended. Angel's feet were rooted to the ground as he watched the smooth landing.

When the propeller stopped turning, he ran to the plane. It was a gorgeous sight—a three-seater biplane with two open cockpits, trimmed for racing and very modern. The pilot climbed out of the front cockpit and jumped from the wing to the ground.

"Hello," she said to Angel, pushing up her goggles to reveal a young and very pretty face. "Quite a crowd here today."

Angel lost his voice, then found it again. "How did you get to fly a brand new Travel Air 4000?" he blurted out.

The pilot grinned at the boy. "I guess you're no farm kid out here in the field," she said. "For your information, a friend of mine asked me to test it out for her. I just took it a short hop from Long Island. Satisfied?"

Angel nodded.

"I'm Katherine Casey," she said, shaking Angel's hand as if he were a grownup. "And you are—" she prompted.

"Angel Rodriguez. I live in Poughkeepsie." Angel had a million questions to ask her—such as, what was she doing here?—but he didn't want to be impolite.

"So, Angel, you know a lot about airplanes, huh?" Katherine walked around her plane, checking the exterior to see how it had weathered the flight. Angel followed her, watching.

"Not as much as I'd like to," he admitted. "I read everything I can get, though. Someday I want to be a pilot."

He touched the propeller blade gently. "Are you a real pilot? With a license and everything?"

"Sure am," answered Katherine proudly. "I'm going to compete in the first Women's Air Derby in August—

we'll fly all the way from Santa Monica, California, to Cleveland, Ohio. Twenty-eight hundred miles, ending up at the National Air Races."

"You mean you're going to fly in the same race as Amelia Earhart?"

"Yep. And Elinor Smith and Pancho Barnes and a bunch of other pilots. Maybe you know their names?"

Angel knew their names, all right. Elinor Smith broke the women's solo endurance record last month with a flight lasting twenty-six hours in the air—and she was only seventeen years old. Angel had seen her picture in the newspaper.

"Elinor Smith can fly under bridges," Angel observed.

"So can I," said Katherine. The pilot grinned mischievously. "Got any bridges around here, Angel?"

"Two," he said. Was she really thinking what he thought she was thinking?

Katherine looked at him, as if she was judging his courage. "Ever flown before?" she asked.

"Haven't had a chance," replied Angel.

"Want to fly now?"

"You bet!" Angel's heart thumped. Could this be happening?

"Then hop in," said Katherine. "How do I get to the bridge?"

"Just follow this road—Route 376. It goes right to Poughkeepsie and you'll see the Hudson River from there."

Angel climbed into the open rear cockpit and put on the pair of goggles. Katherine settled herself at the pilot's controls and threw the ignition switch. The plane thundered to life. Angel took the stone owl out of his pocket and held it for good luck. What would Harold and Miguel say if they could see him now? What would Papa say?

It seemed to Angel as if the plane raced down the field at unbelievable speed. He looked down and saw the ground dropping away. They were in the air!

Angel thought he would burst from happiness. He was flying!

They flew over the white church, which looked like a dollhouse far below. He watched the ploughed fields and blossom-filled apple orchards give way to rows of houses as they got closer to the city. In what seemed like no time at all, he could see the great shining river ahead.

Katherine opened the throttle full-out and the racing plane streaked through the air, heading west across the river. Angel felt himself pressed back against his seat by an enormous invisible force. The power of the engine beneath him was thrilling. He was exhilarated—and not the least bit afraid.

She banked to the left, turning the plane to head back. Angel could see the wing dip toward the earth as the opposite wing rose toward the sky. He held his breath.

Below him was the nearly completed bridge span. The suspension cables were all in place, and the roadbed of the bridge was laid ready for surfacing. Even on Saturday, crews of workmen were busy. They looked so tiny to Angel, flying high above the Hudson.

Katherine shouted something to Angel, but he couldn't hear her over the hum of the engine. The plane took off down the river, going south, and then Katherine turned it again until she was flying straight toward the bridge span.

"I don't believe this!" said Angel aloud. "She's going to fly under the bridge!"

But he was wrong. On the first pass the racing plane buzzed directly over the heads of the workmen on the bridge. Angel could see their surprised and smiling faces as they waved their caps to the silver biplane. Maybe one of them was Papa. They had flown over at such a speed that he couldn't recognize anyone.

On the second pass, Katherine gradually dropped the plane's altitude until it appeared to be only about ten feet above the river. Angel thought he could almost reach down and touch the water.

The huge concrete foundations of the bridge

loomed ahead. Was there truly space enough between them to fly an airplane? And if they made it through, could the plane regain altitude fast enough to avoid the railroad trestle only a short distance to the north?

With a swift acceleration, the Travel Air zoomed between the bridge and the water and pulled up quickly toward the sky. Angel felt as if he were swooping through the air on the back of a great bird.

Katherine took the plane straight up and circled around the bridge once more at high altitude, dipping her wing in salute to the onlookers as she turned back toward the landing field.

Angel was dizzy with joy when the plane touched ground once again on the grassy field.

"How was that for your first flight?" asked Katherine, smiling, as she helped him down from the cockpit. Angel's knees felt weak, but he was happy.

"Maybe we should try the railroad bridge too sometime," he joked.

"You're a born flier, Angel," Katherine said. "Don't lose your dream. If you manage to keep being in the right place at the right time, you might get to fly with Jimmy Doolittle someday."

Jimmy Doolittle was only the most famous racing pilot in America. How could Angel ever meet up with a hero like him?

"Wish me luck in the Nationals," said Katherine as she checked the plane before flying back to Long Island. "This was fun."

Angel still couldn't believe his luck. How could he thank her?

But the young pilot didn't wait for thanks. With a roar of the engine she was airborne and on her way.

Angel watched until the Travel Air was only a pindot of silver in the blue sky. Then he hopped onto his much slower bicycle and peddled homeward.

Papa was already in the kitchen waiting for supper by the time Angel arrived home. The table was set and Mama had cooked red rice and beans, with chicken—one of Angel's favorite meals.

"Angel!" Papa said. "Wait until I tell you what I saw on the bridge today! You'll be so surprised—"

Angel grinned. "I think you'll be the one who is surprised, Papa," he said.

He patted the stone owl in his pocket. Together they had soared through the blue skies today. Somehow Angel knew that, for him, the thrill of flying had just begun.

The daring barnstormers and racing pilots of the 1920s and 1930s set the stage for modern aviation, developing faster and safer aircraft for competition and later for commercial flying. Women pilots such as Elinor Smith proved that they could handle airplanes as well as men could—and they set world records for distance, speed, and endurance. But it wasn't until 1947 that the field on New Hackensack Road officially became the Dutchess County Airport.

12

The Owl and the First Lady

July 1940

On the Fourth of July, Rachel's mother and father took the train to New York City to visit friends. Twelve-year-old Rachel didn't want to go along. Even though the big city was exciting, she wouldn't get to see much of it. She knew from past experience that the grownups would spend the whole day talking in Yiddish about the families they had left behind in Poland and about the war that was destroying Europe. It was too sad a way to spend a holiday.

Rachel wanted to go to a real American Fourth of July celebration, with fireworks and a picnic. She wished that her friend Marie would ask her to spend the day with her. Marie had a backyard with a double wooden swing, where they could sit for hours flipping through movie magazines, and usually there were plenty of Cokes in her refrigerator.

In fact, Rachel had been so sure that Marie would ask her to come over that she had told her mother she had already been invited—otherwise, her parents would have insisted that she go to New York with them. They were coming home on the last train tonight. In the meantime Rachel was stuck in the apartment above the drugstore in the middle of the village of Hyde Park.

Listening to the radio in the kitchen all by herself was boring. She practiced knitting a few rows on the vest she was making, but the wool felt scratchy on a hot July morning. Her mother had straightened up the apartment before she left, so there weren't even any dishes in the sink to wash.

"I've got to get out of here," said Rachel to herself.

Maybe she would walk past Marie's house to see if she was home. Rachel had been brought up to believe that nice girls didn't push themselves where they weren't invited, so she would just have to hope that Marie would notice her walking past and ask her in. Marie's mother was always very pleasant to her, and last week she had asked Rachel which part of Europe she had come from.

"Lodz," Rachel replied. Seeing the blank look on Mrs. Winston's face, she explained, "It's a city in Poland. That's where I was born. We left there four years ago, before the Nazis came."

Rachel had been only eight when her family fled in the middle of the night from Lodz. She remembered almost nothing of the beautiful old city, and she preferred to forget the difficult journey from Poland, which ended at the immigrant processing station at Ellis Island. For weeks she had stared out the window at the Statue of Liberty in New York Harbor—so close it seemed as if she could touch it—asking her mother every day whether the Americans would let them stay.

There was a problem with the paperwork, her mother said. At last they had been allowed to leave the island, and her father had quickly found a job as a welder in a machine shop. In Poland he had been a fine goldsmith.

"That Adolf Hitler is a terrible man," said Mrs. Winston with feeling. "He's got to be stopped before he takes over the whole world."

Rachel hated to think that the German Nazis could win the war they were fighting with the British. But they had already taken over Czechoslovakia and Poland, and now France. She wished that President Roosevelt could do something about it.

The morning sun was warm on her shoulders as she strolled around the corner to Marie's house. She walked along the concrete sidewalk until it ended, just before the small white farmhouse where the Winstons lived. From there the street became more like a country road. Rachel hadn't ever walked the whole length of it, although she knew it came out onto a main road eventually.

There was no sign of life at Marie's house. The front door was shut tight, and the black Buick that Marie's father owned was missing from the driveway. The family must have gone away somewhere for the Fourth of July.

"Not much fun here," said Rachel. She almost wished she had gone with her parents—but not quite.

She decided to go for a walk, maybe as far as the main road. It was a beautiful day, and she enjoyed looking at the colorful flowerbeds of the houses she passed. Nearly every house had an American flag out today.

Rachel had put her own small one in her bedroom window.

When she came to the intersection of the main road, it didn't seem too appealing to turn around and walk back the same way. So she headed south, thinking that she could make a large circle and wind up home again. There wasn't as much to see, mainly fields of hay and stone walls, but Rachel kept walking. She liked her own company and the feeling of being completely on her own.

She was beginning to wonder, though, if there actually were any roads that cut across the fields to take her back to Route 9, where she lived. She hoped she wouldn't have to walk all the way to Poughkeepsie before she found one.

A country lane opened off the main road to the left. Shade trees lined the sides of the dirt road and it looked like such an inviting place that Rachel decided on impulse to go down it. She started down the lane and noticed that her shoelace had come untied. She sat down in the soft grass to retie it.

"Ouch," she said. She was sitting on a hard piece of rock hidden in the grass. She reached to pull it out from beneath her, intending to toss it into the shrubs.

But when Rachel looked at the rock, she saw that it was a piece of limestone. Owl eyes, beak, and feathers were deeply etched into the small stone.

"An owl stone," she whispered aloud. "I wonder how it came here?"

It looked very old, like the great carved stone of the Old City Synagogue at Lodz—she remembered touching the walls when she was a little girl, lifted in her father's arms. Her father had cried when he learned that the German soldiers had completely destroyed the centuries-old synagogue last year.

Rachel continued to stroll along the lane, her attention focused on the little owl in the palm of her hand.

Abruptly she stopped. She heard voices a little way ahead. At the end of the lane she glimpsed a short wooden plank bridge, over a pond surrounded by flowering purple loosestrife and bright orange day lilies.

"Oh no," Rachel thought in a panic. "I've trespassed on someone's private road. They'll probably arrest me." She didn't know whether to run or hide.

But the voices didn't seem to be coming toward her. She saw a stone house with a few black cars parked outside. She took a chance and tiptoed up to the wooden bridge, ready to bolt if anyone saw her.

A group of about fifty people were standing around a tall flagpole on the lawn outside the house. There were men, women, and children gathered in a circle, and an older man sat in a wheelchair reading aloud from a paper in his hand.

With a start, Rachel recognized the man. He was Franklin Delano Roosevelt, President of the United States. She had seen his photograph in the newspaper often enough. And the woman standing beside him was the First Lady, Eleanor Roosevelt. The president's family had lived in Hyde Park for generations.

Rachel thought that she had made a very big mistake. What would her mother say if she found out that her daughter had barged in on the president?

She was close enough now to hear what Mr. Roosevelt was reading. His voice sounded just like it did on the radio.

"We hold these truths to be self-evident; that all men are created equal; that they are endowed by their creator with certain unalienable rights; that among these are life, liberty, and the pursuit of happiness . . ." The president continued to read for a minute, then paused, and said, "The Declaration of Independence, July Fourth, 1776."

All the guests clapped, and the president smiled broadly. He was enjoying himself.

"I would now like to read to you the Preamble to the Constitution of the United States of America."

Rachel stood quietly and listened. When Mr. Roosevelt finished, he went on to talk about the importance of a democratic form of government, where the president, the legislature, and the courts all shared their power to insure fair and equal treatment for every citizen. Sadly, that was not what was occurring in the countries in Europe at this time, he said.

She was so interested in what the president was saying that she leaned far forward over the railing of the wooden bridge, coming into full view of the people gathered around the flagpole. Absentmindedly she thrust her hand deep into the pocket of her skirt, still clasping the stone owl.

Seemingly out of nowhere, three large men in dark suits surrounded her. Two of them held revolvers pointed directly at her, and the other firmly grasped both of her arms so that she was unable to move. She tried to scream but her voice failed her. Who were these men? Why were they going to shoot her?

Rachel was so frightened that she wasn't able to understand what the men were saying. She could see their lips moving but the English sounded like gibberish to her ears. If only she could run to save her life! But the black guns were not toys. Her heart beat like a hammer.

"Let me go," she said, not realizing that she was speaking in Yiddish. To the men it must have sounded like German. "I haven't done anything wrong. It's a mistake."

"Drop the gun," one said.

"What gun?" thought Rachel desperately. "I don't have a gun. *You* have a gun." At least she was thinking in English again.

The man gestured with the barrel of his revolver toward her right hand, clenched around the stone owl in her pocket. "Throw it on the ground," he said.

Confused, Rachel obeyed. Slowly she withdrew her hand from her pocket and tossed the owl onto the wooden bridge in front of her.

The men looked at one another, equally confused. One of them bent to pick up the stone, keeping his gun trained on her all the while. He frowned suspiciously, as if he thought the owl was going to blow up any second.

As scared as she was, the look on the man's face struck her funny. How could anybody be afraid of a little stone owl? Rachel tried not to giggle but she couldn't help herself.

"It's not a gun," she said in clear English. "It's a piece of stone. I found it on the road out there."

The man looked at her keenly. "What's your name, young lady? And what are you doing at Mrs. Roosevelt's private house?"

Rachel suddenly understood. These men were Secret Service agents, assigned to protect the president and his family. And they had thought she was a dangerous intruder, a threat to the president. They weren't going to arrest her if she could explain why she was here. America wasn't like Lodz, where the secret police would come and take people away for questioning, and they never returned.

"I am Rachel Poznanski," she said. "I am twelve years old, I live in Hyde Park, and I am taking a walk on the Fourth of July. I didn't know this road belongs to Mrs. Roosevelt." She took a deep breath to steady her voice. "I am very sorry."

The honesty in her voice must have convinced the agents. They put their guns back into the holsters under their suit jackets.

"We can't be too careful," said the man holding the stone owl. "Even here at Val-Kill there might be someone trying to harm the president. Here's your good luck piece back." He smiled stiffly and handed it to her.

"Since you're already here, would you like to see the rest of the ceremony? They're dedicating the new flagpole today." The agent was trying to be nice to her.

"Oh, yes," she replied eagerly.

The man escorted her to join the crowd and stood

beside her. The ceremony came to a close, the flag was raised, and the people began to sing "God Bless America." Rachel sang too, although her eyes filled with tears. She wasn't sure whether she was happy, proud, or still frightened to death.

Eleanor Roosevelt, wearing a pretty flowered dress, thanked everyone for coming and invited them to stay for ice cream. Rachel wished that she were included. She turned to walk back down to the bridge.

"Rachel! Rachel!"

She couldn't believe that someone was calling her by name here.

Marie bounded across Mrs. Roosevelt's lawn toward her. She looked cool and summery in her shorts and sleeveless blouse.

"What are you doing here?" she asked breathlessly, linking her arm through Rachel's. "I didn't know you knew the president."

"I came in by mistake," Rachel said. "The Secret Service almost shot me."

Marie laughed as if she didn't believe that could happen.

"We're here because Daddy works on the Roosevelt estate," she said. "He takes care of the gardens. Mrs. Roosevelt invited all the staff and their families."

Marie pulled Rachel along with her in the direction of the ice cream.

"I don't want to get in any more trouble. I should go home now," said Rachel.

"Don't be silly. Mrs. Roosevelt won't mind." Marie veered off to the left, where the First Lady stood near the pond, encouraging guests to climb the sloping hill to the house.

"Hello, Mrs. Roosevelt," she said. "I would like you to meet my friend Rachel. She's from Poland but she lives in Hyde Park now. Would it be okay if she stays for ice cream?"

Eleanor Roosevelt looked into Rachel's eyes. Rachel felt almost overwhelmed by the kindness and compassion that came from the older woman. She instantly knew that she was in the presence of someone very special.

"I am so pleased to meet you, Rachel," said Eleanor Roosevelt warmly. "It's lovely that you could join us today. Why don't we walk up together? You can tell me how you like your new home in America."

Rachel realized that Mrs. Roosevelt's interest in her was genuine. As they strolled over the lawn, she found herself describing how different life had been in Poland, where most of the people in the city she knew

were Jewish, like her family, and she had grandparents and aunts and uncles and cousins around every corner. Here in Hyde Park there were people from many countries, of many religions, living in the same community and speaking the same language. Yet among all those people she had no family except her parents.

"I've found that your friends become like family," Eleanor Roosevelt observed quietly. "It is so important to have good friends, and to be one.

"Marie, I'm glad you invited Rachel to come along today," she continued.

"But I didn't," said Marie. You always told the truth to Mrs. Roosevelt. "She came here by accident."

The First Lady looked at Rachel, puzzled. Rachel looked down at her toes. Now she would probably be asked to leave, without even tasting the ice cream. But first she would explain about the road, the Secret Service men, and the stone owl.

Marie's mouth hung open with surprise.

"May I see the owl?" asked Mrs. Roosevelt.

Rachel nodded and held out her palm to the First Lady. The stone owl sat comfortably, its eyes old and wise.

Eleanor Roosevelt, wiser still, held the owl respectfully in her hand for a moment and then returned it to Rachel. "What an interesting visitor," she said, smiling. "It's been quite a Fourth of July. This morning we had some handsome young pilots from the Air Corps drop in for breakfast—and now we have a stone owl. I can't even guess who will show up this afternoon." She didn't seem to mind at all.

She gestured to the dishes of ice cream set out on tables on the patio. "Vanilla or chocolate, my dears? Help yourselves."

Rachel and Marie sat under the shade of a large lilac bush to eat their ice cream. It tasted creamy, sweet, and delicious.

"You mean you walked all the way here?" asked Marie, as if she had just figured it out.

Rachel nodded. "I started out to see if you were home, and then I kept on walking." She sighed. "I'm not looking forward to the return trip, though. My feet already have blisters."

"Silly," said Marie. "You can ride in the car with us. Even better, I'll ask my mom if you can stay for the afternoon and then come to the fireworks display tonight! Won't that be fun?"

"It will be the most exciting Fourth of July ever," replied Rachel. She licked the last drop of chocolate ice cream from her spoon.

Eleanor Roosevelt was the wife of President Franklin D. Roosevelt and the niece of President Theodore Roosevelt. President Harry S Truman called her the "First Lady of the World." Although she loved her quiet retreat at Val-Kill, she devoted her life to improving the welfare of all humankind, and she brought a personal energy and vision to her work that has never been equaled. In 1946 she became the United States delegate to the United Nations, which was formed after the end of World War II to promote peace and security throughout the world, and was the chairperson of its Commission for Human Rights.

Sailing on the *Clearwater*

August 1969

Fourteen-year-old Daniel Chao stood on the bank of the Hudson, his eyes fastened on a sloop with white sails proudly making her way downriver. He had never seen a real sloop before. It looked like a picture out of a history book.

A few motorboats chugged by, cutting wakes through the murky water that sloshed against the rocks at Daniel's feet. The ripples barely moved the black automobile tire lying half-submerged on the muddy riverbank.

"Hey! Lee Ann! Don't touch that junk!" Daniel sighed and scrambled down the rocks until he reached the four-year-old girl. She was about to pluck a chewed-up rubber ball from the river where it floated, temptingly, among the discarded soda cans.

"It's filthy," he said. "Nasty. It'll give you germs. Got it?"

The little girl looked up at him and smiled. Her shiny black hair was straight and neat, her bangs pinned back with a pretty barrette. Her ruffled pink dress was covered with dark sludge where she had wiped her hands dry.

"Oh no," groaned Daniel. "Your mother will kill me. What did you do to your dress?"

Lee Ann didn't say anything but instead pointed to her feet. Her sandals were soaking wet and greasy dark splashes of water stained her white socks.

"I chased a pigeon," she said. "And I almost fell in over there." She nodded toward a pile of rocks and jagged concrete overgrown with slippery green algae.

"You know you're not supposed to go in the river. It's not safe for swimming," Daniel said sternly.

"Sorry," said Lee Ann. But she didn't sound the least bit sorry.

Daniel sighed again. "If anybody around here is sorry, it's me," he said to himself under his breath. "Sorry I ever agreed to babysit this kid."

Sometimes a good deed backfires in your face. When Mrs. Wang asked him if he could just take Lee Ann to the park for a few hours this afternoon while she went to a meeting, it didn't seem an impossible favor. But Lee Ann was smart and she was fast, too. Daniel was looking forward to five o'clock, when at last he could take her home.

Aloud, in as cheerful a voice as he could manage, he said, "Come on, let's go and watch the boat coming in. She's called the *Clearwater*."

Lee Ann wrinkled her nose. "Dirty water, dirty water, dirty water," she sang at the top of her lungs as she followed Daniel over to the weather-beaten dock.

The crew had furled the sloop's massive mainsail

and they used ropes as thick as Lee Ann's wrist to fasten the sloop to its mooring. She was a beautiful vessel, over a hundred feet long and made of wood. The white-tipped mast was more than a hundred feet tall. It seemed to Daniel that the webs of rope rigging stretched from the deck to the sky.

A group of people had gathered, and Daniel could see more people walking down Main Street toward the park. As he and Lee Ann watched, the crew of the sloop began to carry guitars, African drums, and other instruments from the dock to the grassy center of the park.

"They don't look like sailors," observed Lee Ann. "They look like people."

Daniel had to admit that she was right. The crew wore tee shirts and shorts, bluejeans and brightly colored bandannas. Some of the men had long hair and beards. Some of the women looked as old as his mother. But they were all smiling and waving at the crowd.

The crew set up a makeshift stage area with wooden crates and barrels from the deck. Many of the people in the crowd applauded when a tanned, wiry fellow wearing a Greek fisherman's cap and a trim beard stepped into the center of the circle, a banjo in his hand.

"That's Pete Seeger, the folksinger activist," said an older girl sitting next to Daniel on the grass. "Building the *Clearwater* was his idea in the first place."

The girl had long blonde hair, round gold-rimmed glasses, and purple bellbottom pants. On a leather thong around her neck hung a peace symbol. Daniel

132

thought maybe she was a hippie, a flower child like the ones at the Woodstock festival last week. Peace and love for everybody—this girl even seemed to like Lee Ann, who was tickling her bare foot with a blade of grass.

"Welcome, everybody," said a tall man with a bushy mustache and curly hair bleached by the sun. He stood next to Pete Seeger. "We're glad to see you down here. It's a beautiful day. And this used to be a beautiful river."

He gestured toward the sloop, riding gently on the water. "The *Clearwater* is an accurate replica of the sloops that sailed the Hudson in the nineteenth century. She was launched this summer in South Bristol, Maine, with an all-volunteer crew. Lots of us are folksingers, and some of us have never sailed a boat before. It's been exciting." He laughed and then became serious. "We've sailed down the New England coast and up the Hudson as far as Albany. Unlike a hundred years ago, now we sail on a river polluted by sewage, garbage, and toxic chemicals. Down by New York City you can even see the toilet waste floating by."

Daniel thought that was unbelievably disgusting. No wonder they couldn't swim in it.

"We're hoping that by sailing the *Clearwater* up and down the Hudson, people might get some ideas about cleaning up the waterways. We can do it—if we all work together. The sloop is just the beginning."

The man grinned at Pete and the other musicians, waiting with their instruments. "Now we're gonna sing some songs and play some music and ask you all to join in—not just with the singing, but with helping to bring back this wonderful river."

A young woman in the crowd called out in a hopeful voice, "If we can put an astronaut on the moon, we ought to be able to clean up a river on our own planet!" Only last month, Neil Armstrong had been the first person to walk on the moon. Daniel had watched it on television.

The audience cheered and clapped, and the music began. Folk songs, Irish songs, sea chanties, songs about the river, songs about peace and justice. The girl next to Daniel stood up and sang along, swaying to the rhythm of the drums. Everyone was smiling and children were dancing on the grass.

But all of a sudden Daniel realized something was wrong. Where was Lee Ann?

The little girl had disappeared.

He squinted his eyes to see if he could spot her among the group of children. She wasn't there.

He ran over to the rocks near the water, where she had slipped earlier, calling her name. He was beginning to get nervous. But there was no sign that she had been there.

A black woman with Afro-style hair sat quietly on the grass, watching her two small children throw stones into the water.

"Excuse me, but did you see a little girl in a pink dress near here?" Daniel asked anxiously. "Maybe a few minutes ago?"

"No, I didn't," replied the woman. "I've been here for a while now, since the music started. No one's been near the water."

"Thanks anyway," Daniel said. At least that meant Lee Ann hadn't fallen into the river. Yet. But he had to find her.

Daniel searched the crowd of people, looking desperately for a glimpse of pink ruffles about three feet tall. He thought of asking the blonde hippie girl if she had noticed where Lee Ann went, but he couldn't find her either.

The concert had ended and a young boy was passing among the throngs of people, carrying a small barrel. People tossed dollar bills and silver coins into the barrel. The money they collected would feed the crew and keep the *Clearwater* sailing.

If Daniel had any money, he would have put it into the barrel—but of course if he had any money, then he wouldn't have taken this stupid babysitting job. And Lee Ann wouldn't have gotten lost.

"You haven't seen a little lost kid in a pink dress, have you?" he asked the boy with the barrel.

"Nope," said the boy. "But you can ask that guy over there. He's the captain. Maybe he can help find her."

Daniel was embarrassed to tell the sloop captain that the child he was supposed to be watching had disappeared, but he was more afraid than he would admit, even to himself. Suppose she had been kidnapped? Or had run away? She was his responsibility, and he had blown it.

The captain smiled and told Daniel not to worry. They would find Lee Ann. He spoke briefly to a few crew members, who fanned out through the crowd, asking people if they had seen a four-year-old girl in a pink dress. Daniel walked over toward the dock, thinking that maybe Lee Ann had wanted to see the boat up close.

As he stepped onto the dock, his stomach lurched. Floating in the deep oily water near the pilings was a small white sandal. Lee Ann's sandal.

He thundered down the wooden planks toward the sloop. There had to be someone on board.

"Help!" he shouted. "Quick! Help!"

A head popped up from below the deck. "What's wrong?" the woman shouted as she hoisted herself up the ladder.

Daniel pointed wildly over the side of the dock. "Drowned!" he said, barely able to get the word out.

The woman rushed to look over the side of the rail. "Who drowned?" she cried.

"Lee Ann. Little girl—her sandal—" Daniel was horrified. It was all his fault. He should never have let go of her hand.

"Lee Ann?" the woman said loudly.

"What?" answered Lee Ann herself, climbing up from the top of the ladder to the deck. Her pink dress was even dirtier but she looked the picture of health. She was eating an apple and staring at Daniel.

"We found your sandal," said the woman drily. "And your friend, I think."

She held out a strong hand to Daniel. "Hop aboard, kid," she said. "You look like you could use a drink."

Daniel sat down weakly on a coil of rope.

"Thanks," he said automatically when Tammy handed him a paper cup of water. "I've been looking all over for her. I thought, when I saw the sandal, that—"

"Well, you were close," she said. "When I caught up with little Miss Lee Ann here, she was ten feet up in the rigging and heading for the crow's nest. She lost her sandal when I brought her down."

"Sorry," said Lee Ann.

"I'm giving up babysitting. There must be an easier way to earn money," Daniel said.

"I'm sure there is," agreed Tammy. "I was just waiting for the captain to come back so I could return Lee Ann to the person who brought her here. She's got more energy than I can handle."

She winked at the little girl. Lee Ann tried to wink

back. Clearly they had been practicing.

The captain and two other crew members appeared on the dock, looking concerned.

Daniel stood up and waved from the deck of the sloop. "She's here," he called out. "We found her. It's okay now."

The captain gave him a thumbs-up and turned to go back to tell the others.

"You scared a lot of people, Lee Ann," Daniel said. "Not just me, but the crew and everybody else who was looking for you. You shouldn't have run off without telling me."

Lee Ann hung her head. "Do I have to go home now?"

"Definitely," said Daniel.

"Can I come to see the *Clearwater* again sometime?"

"Of course," said Tammy.

"Ask your mother," said Daniel at the same time. They laughed.

"Are you sure you can manage to get her home safely?" Tammy certainly had gotten to know Lee Ann.

"I think I'll carry her," Daniel replied. "Want a piggyback ride, Lee Ann?"

The little girl nodded happily.

"At least I'll know where she is," he explained to Tammy as she helped him off the sloop.

Lee Ann rode comfortably on Daniel's shoulders as he crossed the park and walked back to the neighborhood where they lived. Daniel hoped that she wouldn't do anything horrible to his hair while she was up there.

She kept her arms wrapped around his neck but she didn't try to strangle him, not even once.

When they got to the Wangs' house, he gently let her down to the sidewalk. She was missing a sandal and her clothes were a mess. He would have to explain to Mrs. Wang what had happened. This was the end of his babysitting career, without a doubt.

"Daniel," whispered Lee Ann. "Thank you for taking me to see the big boat. I didn't mean to run away and scare you."

He was surprised. That was the closest to a real apology from Lee Ann that he had ever heard. But there was more.

"I have a present for you," she said. Usually Lee Ann's presents were spit-out pieces of chewing gum or already-licked lollipops. Daniel couldn't wait.

"Tammy on the boat gave it to me, and I'm giving it to you. For keeps," she said.

Into Daniel's outstretched hand she dropped a small stone. It was carved to look like an owl, with round eyes and a beak. Daniel could see deep scored lines that looked like feathers.

"Wow," said Daniel. What a present from a four-year-old. "Are you sure you want me to have it?"

Lee Ann nodded. "Tammy said I could give it to somebody I like a lot, if I wanted to. That's why she gave it to me. Because she likes me." Lee Ann was pleased to have made a friend.

"Where did Tammy get it?" Daniel asked, curious.

"She said she found it in the barrel where they collect the money for the *Clearwater*. She said maybe

139

somebody put it in for good luck. You can't spend it, though."

"I know," said Daniel. "I'll keep it for a long long time. Thanks, Lee Ann. That was nice of you." He pushed the doorbell buzzer with his thumb.

Maybe there was hope for the kid yet.

The sloop Clearwater *and her volunteer crews have been sailing up and down the Hudson River for over twenty-five years now, becoming a "Classroom of the Waves" to promote ecological understanding and to teach people about environmental laws and how to be effective citizens. Tires and garbage no longer float past Poughkeepsie, and the water is clear enough to see through. But the river at New York City and Albany is still polluted by toxic chemicals and industrial waste discharge, and the fish aren't safe to eat. Our precious planet Earth needs our help to survive and be healthy once again. The* Clearwater *brings a message of hope to all of us.*

A Note from the Author

Dark Moon could never have guessed that the owl he carved from a piece of limestone nearly four hundred years ago would have so many adventures in Dutchess County.

The stories that take place in this 800-square-mile county are just a small part of what makes up the history of America. Every community has its own stories and its own important place in our nation and in our world.

Owl's Journey gives you a glimpse into the daily lives of people just like you, throughout the centuries. Some of those people are real, and some of them are fictional characters who appeared in my imagination as if they were real. (If you truly want to know who the real people are, write to me and I'll send you a list.)

As this book ends, the stone owl has just returned from sailing on the *Clearwater* to clean up the Hudson River. You might want to continue the story now on your own. Who knows where the stone owl could turn up next?

Acknowledgments

Writing *Owl's Journey* has been, for me, a labor of love. My great-great-great-great-great-grandfather Kasparus Westervelt came to Dutchess County from Holland (via Hackensack, New Jersey) in 1744, and the house where I now live is very near the 1,600 acres he bought between the Hudson River and the Wappingers Creek, part of the original Rombout Patent. My great-great-grandfather Lorenzo Van Buren owned a brickyard at Fishkill Landing, and my great-grandmother Elizabeth Westervelt Van Buren taught in the one-room schoolhouse in Spackenkill, just outside Poughkeepsie. My great-grandmother on my father's side, Mary Bridget Butler Dibble, emigrated to America from County Clare in Ireland more than a hundred years ago. I thank all my family, especially my mother, Beverly Van Buren Shaw, for the gift of life in this beautiful, historic Hudson Valley.

I could not have written this book without the support of my dear friends Cait Johnson, Julie Kessler, Harriet Schwartz, and Joyce Townsend. Their enthusiasm for the project—and the occasional gift of an owl card or figure to keep me inspired—has been wonderful. I am very grateful for their friendship.

Many other people have given generously of their time, research materials, and advice. I particularly would like to acknowledge the assistance of Eileen M. Hayden of the Dutchess County Historical Society in the earlier stages of the book. Debra Zwillinger has helped in more areas than I can even count. I would like to thank Donald A. Schoudel for material on iron ore mines; Jack Maguire for his ideas on storytelling; Fawn Tantillo for her expert knowledge of the fish in the Hudson; Len Tantillo for helping to find just the right airplanes; Judy Presson for her good humor despite fairly impossible deadlines; Virginia C. Drews for the gift of a special book; and Rhianna Mirabello for the loan of her owl. The staff members of the LaGrange Association Library and the Adriance Memorial Library were very helpful, as were the people at Madame Brett's Homestead in Beacon, the Beacon Historical Society, the Eleanor Roosevelt National Historic Site at Val-Kill, and the Hudson River Sloop Clearwater organization.

My husband, Joe Tantillo, has my enduring love and gratitude for putting up with me while I lived in four different centuries at the same time, as well as my admiration for the lovely sketches that illustrate the stories. I hope that our son, Nick Tantillo, will come to appreciate the bravery and beauty of the history that happened on the river and the land in Dutchess County.

Maura D. Shaw

If you would like to purchase another copy of *Owl's Journey: Four Centuries of an American County* and you cannot find it in your local bookstore, please send a check or money order for $15.95 (plus $3.00 shipping and handling charge for the first book, and $.75 for each additional book—New York State residents add sales tax) to:

The Shawangunk Press
8 Laurel Park
Wappingers Falls, NY 12590

Wholesaler and distributor queries are welcome.